PRAISE FOR THE

"Dr. Xa Xiong's story reads like a movie script. His ventures from a small village in Laos to the bustling city life of America is truly amazing. His vow to God is an underlying force that goes beyond human determination in his quest to become a doctor. This is the essential drive that ultimately leads to Dr Xiong's achievements. The fact that he attained his goal and became a medical doctor in a new and vastly different culture points to something more than human endeavor. May you discover what that essential drive was as you search the pages of this exceptional book."

—Steven D Miles, Pastor and author of *By What Authority*

"Dr. Xa Xiong's life story should be inspirational to all who aspire to achieve what may seem impossible. As an eye-witness to the Hmong people's experiences of war, displacement, and migration across the globe, his lived experiences of overcoming an enormous amount of obstacles to become a medical doctor is a prime example of human resiliency."

—Chia Youyee Vang, PhD, Associate Professor and author of *Hmong America: Reconstructing Community in Diaspora*

"Dr. Xa Xiong's trek of becoming the man he is today will trigger and influence you to never give up. The little boy, who started from nowhere, became a meritorious, self-made man through strength, faith, and dedication. This book will influence and move your soul to an optimal state of mind."

—Yeng Eric Xiong, DC, Chiropractic Physician

"The Impossible Dream" by Dr. Xa Xiong is truly an inspirational read. Faced with intense ongoing struggles, Dr. Xa Xiong strives through them with grace. He portrays a kind soul with resilience and determination. His love of the Lord and his family is clearly the strength that has driven him toward his success. A true role-model in the making. Education has always been an important factor in my life. I find this book to be encouraging to myself and possibly to any student or student to be, to not give up and always excel to your fullest potential. "Education is the key to success", Dr. Xa Xiong."

—Mary Yang, BS—Biology

"Anyone who has grown up with tragedy starting from a young age and has felt a sense of defeat in this life should read Dr. Xiong's book. His life demonstrates that even someone who grew up in a remote part of the world and has experienced some of life's worse happenings could achieve his dreams. Dr. Xiong's story is a perfect example that success does not only have to happen for those who have been born into money or higher education. Determination, motivation, handwork, and a belief in ones abilities to achieve anything this world has to offer may be all that it takes to actualize one's dreams. Dr. Xiong's willingness to share his life with the world is a testament to his desire for others to achieve as well. He is a role model for us all."

—Maysee Yang Herr, PhD, Associate Professor

THE IMPOSSIBLE DREAM
Memoirs of a Refugee Boy

The journey of a refugee boy who made a promise to his beloved brother with the impossible dream of becoming a medical doctor and healing the hearts of others.

FOREWORD

I first met Dr. Xiong in a walk-in clinic, where he worked as a physician. His gentle, friendly manner caught my attention immediately, and over the next few weeks and months I heard the fascinating story of his family's escape from Laos following the Vietnam War. The tale of his journey, as well as his determination to become a doctor against all odds inspires considerable admiration. Be prepared for a thrilling tale of courage and adventure as you follow a young boy through the jungles of Laos and Thailand all the way to the bright lights of California, Alaska, the Caribbean, and finally, the quiet hills and countryside of Wisconsin, where today that young boy, now grown, serves his community with faithfulness and compassion. You must read The Impossible Dream!

—Claudia Smith, Retired Editor

The impossible dream is nothing short of incredible! In this wonderful book you will be inspired to follow your own dreams no matter how big they may seem. Dr Xa Xiong shares with the reader that nothing is impossible no matter what your circumstances are or where you are from. You will also discover that no dream is too big when you follow your heart and practice persistence. His love for his family is evident throughout this amazing book and was a driving force to accomplish the impossible dream.

Dr Xiong I thank you for writing this wonderful book and helping others follow their dreams.

—Forrest Willett, *#1 Bestselling Author of Baseballs Don't Bounce: A Journey from Hopelessness to Happiness*

How do you measure the strength of a young boy's promise to his dying brother? A Hmong Paj ntaub (story cloth) tells the journey of the people from a village life, through war, flight through the jungle, crossing the Mekong River, refugee camps in Thailand, the airplane flight to the strange new country of America. It is my privilege to have worked with Xa Xiong at Kajsiab House, a NIMH Best Practice Model Program for cross cultural healing from the trauma of war and refugee flight. When we ask why America needs refugees, it is because Dr. Xa Xiong, who brings his dreams through that long journey, is the kind of person who makes America strong. He is a credit to his family, the Hmong people and the Dream of America. Even knowing the story, I could not put the book down until I had read it cover to cover.

—Frederick W Coleman, MD

Dr. Xa Xiong's long odyssey as a refugee boy, fleeing the chaos of war in Laos to become a medical doctor in the United States, spans decades and continents. This undefended and personal account is a piece of living history. It illustrates his own determination and hard work, as well as some of the best aspects of Hmong culture: support from the family, respect for tradition, the value of listening to one's elders and sacrifice of the individual for the good of everyone. I recommend this fascinating account of the refugee experience as an example of the triumph of the human spirit.

—Roger Garms, PhD

THE Impossible DREAM

DEDICATION

This book is dedicated to my father—Captain Yong Ge Xiong, my mother—Yer-Kue Hang, my wife—Choua Yang, my brother Pao, my sister Phoua, my children: Elizabeth, Einstein, Emily, Elena, Alexander, my brothers, my sisters, and everyone who believed in me to achieve the best things in life.

CONTENTS

THE Impossible DREAM

ACKNOWLEDGMENTS

This book would not be possible without the encouragement and support from the individuals who have touched my life. Thank you God, Mother Nature and our Ancestors for blessing me with the capability to achieve the impossible dream of becoming a medical doctor with the ability to heal many people. I would also like to thank my wonderful family and friends for their love and motivation, Claudia and Donnie Smith for helping me with transcribing and editing my first publication, Pastor Steven and Phyllis Miles for second editing, and the teachers and mentors in my life, who influenced me and believed in me.

INTRODUCTION

God's hand brushed away the clouds, and the lush mountains appeared. A hidden village named Long Cheng was home to the Hmong natives. Scattered across the green hills were huts built with wooden poles and wavy aluminum facades and roofing. The patter of bare feet played upon the ground. Mothers and their children traveled many miles to harvest their next meal while the fathers joined the army and allied with the United States of America to fight for freedom. This village was never a peaceful one. Everyone was an early bird, waking up just before the sunrise to the rooster's crow. Clusters of lousy, unsanitary street vendors tried to make ends meet. In the very streets where children played, trash littered the corners while the stray animals searched for scraps. Recreational activities and education were not huge objectives in Long Cheng. In this impoverished place, the main objective was to survive the Secret War. Long Cheng surrounded a military base from which the American and Hmong Air Force battled the Communists. The Hmong were in agreement to stop the flow of North Vietnamese troops and supplies through the Ho Chi Minh Trail along Southeastern Laos, rescue American pilots that were shot down, and protect the US Air Force navigation radar in Phou Pha Thi that guided the B52-s and the jets bombing military targets in North Vietnam. In return for their service and loyalty, the Hmong were promised safety and freedom. This became the catalyst of the most conflictive and bloody war in all history for the Hmong.

As a result of the Vietnam War, the Hmong were no longer safe in their own homes. During the cold nights while the crickets chirped, the communists would advance closer to the village. They carried their guns, raided homes, harmed innocent lives, and persecuted the Hmong because of their affiliation with the United States of America. I was only six years old when Saigon fell and my family began the long journey from Laos to Thailand, and then to the land of the free—the United States of America. I faced numerous dangers with formidable obstacles, crossing treacherous paths, and living under dreadful conditions in refugee camps.

Indelible memories repeatedly flashed in my mind, and a promise I made to my beloved brother scarred my heart forever, inspiring my journey as a refugee who not only had a dream, but became the dream.

After many days of travel huddled in the rear of an old truck, we finally found ourselves outside of a towering wired gate. We arrived at the Nong Khai Refugee Camp in Thailand early in the morning. The security guards watched the campground carefully with their piercing gazes. After many hours of waiting, we were directed to settle in an open field away from the compartment homes. Mud tracks paved the dirt roads and smoke filled the air. In the camp, thousands of Hmong crammed together into long buildings, separated into small sub-compartments. Families bonded with one another, cooking what always looked to be their last meal. Life in the refugee camp was not a place for children. Food and water were limited for each household. On many occasions, my parents steamed grass in water to satisfy our empty stomachs. The lack of sanitation and medical resources were the main causes of illness and death in these camps.

One hot summer day, my older brother, Pao, came home after a long morning of fishing. The guards did not notice him leave the campsite and it was another successful catch of the day for him. My mother scaled the fish and prepared supper for the night. As the family gathered around the poorly made straw table to eat, I noticed my older brother was not present. Pao was asleep and did not awaken. He began to sweat profusely, gasping for air. We watched him struggle to relieve the unbearable pressure upon his lungs. After exhausting all of the traditional Hmong treatments, nothing prevailed and Pao only got worse. Every day, I would sit at the end of his bed in the hopes that Pao would open his eyes and say something. Days passed, and there was no improvement. My parents finally took Pao to the refugee health center but nothing could be done. After many hours of filling out papers, we were able to leave the campground to go to the nearest Thai hospital. Without any money for transportation, my parents had to borrow from close relatives for a taxi. As we traveled, Pao's thin body began to perspire. Beads of sweat spread throughout his body like a virus and his breathing became heavier and sporadic.

When we finally arrived at the hospital, my father gathered Pao in his arms and ran into the emergency room where no one greeted us. After a long wait, a nurse assigned us to one of the stretchers by the window, but no doctor came to see my brother. Medical tools and medicine abounded in this hospital, and yet the ones who studied to become the wielders of these lifesaving instruments did not appear.

For what seemed like hours, we waited until a nurse finally arrived. After a simple glance at his thin feeble body, she said there was nothing they could do to help him. Grasping my older brother's trembling hand, I promised him that I would fulfill the impossible dream of becoming a medical doctor so I could heal the hearts of others and place hope in their eyes. Pao's fingers loosened as he took his last labored breath. Life would never be the same.

CHAPTER ONE

The Family

The Family

In 1968 the chaos of the Vietnam War filled the warm air. In the United States, Lyndon Johnson was President, and in Laos, General Vang Pao was Commander in Chief of Military Region 2 (MR2) in Long Cheng. During this time, my father underwent training for the police force stationed in Vientiane, located on the banks of the Mekong River bordering Thailand. The rest of my family, including my mother and older brothers, lived in a small home made from aluminum on the hillside of Long Cheng. My mother gave birth to me on a Sunday morning when the sun peaked over the mountain tops and the rooster crowed, awakening the silent village. I was given the name Law Xang after the youngest brother of an ancient Hmong folktale. Law Toua, Law Lue, and Law Xang were mythical heroes who fought courageously against wild beasts that captured and caused harm to the villagers. The brave warriors brought loved ones back to their families and restored peace to the land. My father was very fond of this folktale and he named my brothers and me after these legendary defenders.

5

My father, Yong Ge Xiong, was born in 1947 in one of the lowland provinces of Laos. He was the first son of Xao Ying Xiong and Lu Thao. They had a large family and lived in a small house made from tree trunks and mud. Together, they slept side-by-side on a strapped hay bed elevated with the support of four wooden legs. Every morning before the sunrise, they would haul their bamboo baskets onto their backs and journey along the dirt road and woods to work on the farm. The heavy bamboo baskets were filled with farming tools, seeds, and sometimes if they were lucky, a small handful of rice wrapped in a banana leaf for lunch. They worked many hours farming on the small patch of land to provide food for the family. They lived the majority of their lives in poverty with limited food supplies and no financial advantages. Although life was difficult to begin with, my father's family encountered more hardship when the Vietnam War intensified in 1955.

At the age of 13, my father was recruited into the Royal Lao Army. He barely had the strength to carry a weapon, yet was sent into the army to protect his country. What he experienced changed his life forever. He was trained to fight fearlessly during combat in order to protect his family and his country, in hopes that it would bring peace to the homeland. After many years of fighting for his country with support from the United States, my father resigned from the army and joined the Royal Lao Police in 1968 to train in the police academy camp in Vientiane. His unit was the second police platoon to be trained under the Royal Thai Police—Police Aerial Resupply Unit (PARU). The Royal Lao Police

Academy in Vientiane was recognized as one of the most intense training programs that existed in Laos during that time. My father was one of the few great men who graduated from the academy with The Royal Lao Police rank of Loei Eek—Captain (three five-pointed gold stars). My father was sent to station in Long Cheng. He was a man of high integrity, a brave leader, and a true patriot to his country. He was one of the very first in our patrilineal family to learn how to read, write, and speak the Laotian language in addition to our native Hmong tongue. He encouraged his younger siblings to go to school and be the very best they could be. He would often say, "Education is the key to becoming a successful person."

A Great Nurturing Mother

My mother—Yer was born to Xai Her Kue and Youa Yang. When she was only three days old, her father passed away, making a huge impact on her life. Her mother remarried and as a result my mother endured many hardships and struggled to maintain a healthy childhood. She did not have a stable place to call home. She bounced from one household to another and as she grew older she was accepted only because of her ability to nurture children, cook, and clean. In return, the families provided food and a roof for shelter. Although she endured many hurdles, she survived her difficult childhood, grew up to be a beautiful woman, and eventually married my father. When she brought me into this world, she taught me the value of family and always brightened our home with the sound of her laughter. She loved me very much.

One day, I wandered into the street markets in our village and saw a short-sleeved white dress shirt with clear buttons that ran down the midline seam. In my head, I could imagine all the children circling me and complimenting how cool my shirt looked. I rushed home and immediately demanded that my mom buy the shirt for me.

She looked at me with her concerned eyes and said, "Son, we cannot afford to buy the shirt."

In anger, I stormed out of the house and ran away. My mother followed me for a while and the closer she approached the faster and farther I ran. Eventually, she stopped, placed her hands on her knees, and tried to catch her breath, she threatened to kill herself if I didn't stop running. I abruptly stopped in my tracks in fear of losing her. She grabbed me by the arm and I embarrassingly stared at the ground, afraid to look into her distressed eyes.

Tears ran down my face as she held me tight and told me, "Son, we do not have money right now, but I will work hard and even sell my valuable jewelry to buy you the shirt."

I rubbed my eyes and told her how sorry I was. My mother's heart was full of forgiveness for any mistake—big or small—that I made. She was my drive for success and I could never thank her enough for the love and sacrifices she made for me.

Throughout my schooling years, over a thousand times, when I faced academic challenges, I would always hear her say, "Education is created by humans and not by evil...it is learnable."

The Fall of Long Cheng, Laos

We were stationed in Long Cheng—Military Region 2 (MR2), commanded by General Vang Pao. Some of my father's many duties were to patrol General Vang Pao's Home, the Military Zone 2 Airbase, and the Royal Lao King's summer house. In addition, he worked in the crime investigation and intervention unit, and served as a food inspector. In 1972, more than a dozen deputies worked under my father's command. My father always knew that the key to lifelong survival and the achievement of high political rank was education. As soon as I could stretch my right fingers over my head to touch my left ear, my father sent me to elementary school in Long Cheng, where I started as a first grader. It was the summer of 1974, and I was nearly six years old. The chaos of the Vietnam War escalated to a boiling point and civilians as well as military men and women were killed in action on a daily basis. Every time we heard the H-34 helicopter fly over our heads, we knew right away that someone's husband, wife, son, or daughter had been killed in action. Sadness and mourning swallowed the happiness in the village. Frequently we heard the grunts and heaves of the soldiers carrying the deceased fighters. Respectfully, their bodies were laid in several rows, enclosed in body bags or covered with white or green nylon sheets. We would hear family members sobbing hysterically as they grieved for their loved ones. These vicious memories were engraved in my mind forever.

The Vietnam War intensified so immensely that our lives were no longer safe. A series of attacks advanced closer to Long Cheng until finally there was no choice but to leave the country.

CHAPTER TWO

Exodus to Thailand and Refugee Camps

Exodus to Thailand

On April 30, 1975 Communism caused the fall of Saigon. The Communists came to power and dethroned the Royal Laos government. The United States CIA Officials evacuated from Long Cheng. Our lives were no longer safe, and we were in danger of imprisonment and persecution. My father's life was immensely threatened because he had served the United States under the command of General Vang Pao and The United States Central Intelligence Agency (CIA).

My father sought every opportunity to help us flee from Laos. Due to his affiliation with law enforcement, he overheard that the U.S. C-46 evacuation planes had been landing in the Long Cheng MR2 Airbase. Many Hmong people had fled from Laos to Thailand since the 12th of May, and there was only one more flight departing on May 14th, 1975. Thousands of Hmong waited with fear and confusion for several days in an open airstrip, hoping to board the U.S. C-130 plane. Our family joined them in hopes of boarding the last flight to liberation.

11

There were about 20 people in our family among the rest of the Hmong who slept bundled up in groups in the midst of a cold breeze. On the morning of May 14, 1975, gun shots were fired by the enemy in the far distance as we listened quietly for the sound of the airplane to arrive. Everyone continued to look up into the sky in hopes of spotting the bird that would fly us away from harm and danger. Finally, we heard a loud booming engine and propeller in the distance. Everyone looked up and we saw a gigantic airplane approaching the airfield. As the plane landed and taxied closer, people started running towards the open field in panic, fear, and desperation.

My father said, "Let's get our things and start walking."

The strong wind from the airplane blew in my face as I tried to keep my eyes open. Dust filled the air as the airplane slowly taxied up the runway. The cargo door opened, and everyone rushed to board the aircraft while it was still taxiing. My mother grabbed my wrist along with my sister's. Pushing and shoving through the crowd, we were able to climb up the cargo door with our belongings. At that very moment, my father turned around to glance at Long Cheng for one last time, and unexpectedly he spotted our grandma lost among the crowd on the pavement of the airfield. My father immediately retrieved all of us and told us to get off the plane.

We ran to our grandma and by the time we had reached her and turned around, the doors were already shut. I could sense my father's disappointment and sadness as he pushed the family away from the departing plane. Our dreams and hopes for a new life dissipated before our eyes. We were told to stay away from the runway and in misery we watched as the last evacuation airplane taxied down the runway and eventually lifted off from the Long Cheng MR2 Airbase. Thousands of Hmong, including our family, were left behind enemy lines. People were crying and imploring God, Mother Nature, and Ancestors everywhere in hope of aid. There was no response except from the remnants of the endangered Hmong left behind.

As the plane disappeared into the blue sky, we quickly gathered our belongings and walked away from the airfield. We reached my uncle's military vehicle parked two miles off base and my dad grabbed me under my arms and lifted me into the truck. We took a long bumpy ride from Long Cheng to Vientiane. I saw the clouds of dust trailing behind as we trekked into the silent night, and my mom held me close. No one spoke a word and I soon sank into a deep sleep. I awoke to the sound of people. We had arrived in Vang Vieng where we stayed for several days. My father heard that thousands of Hmong waited in a valley one mile north of the Hin Heup Bridge to cross over to Vientiane. We got back to my uncle's truck and took the bumpy ride to the valley. As we were approaching the valley, the dirt road became narrow and crowds of people swarmed our truck. We were no longer able to drive on the road, so we climbed down from the truck, pulling with us all our belongings— bamboo carrying baskets, military canteens, blankets, bed sheets, pots, pans, and spoons. We carried everything on our backs, and began the long journey to the Hin Heup Bridge, joining with many other Hmong families. We all shared one vision: asylum and a new beginning. Along the way, we saw many adults, children, and babies resting on the side of the road, hidden under trees and bushes and handmade banana leaf huts. There were scattered fires emitting black smoke, which gleefully danced in the hot summer air and then dissipated into the heavens. The temperature had soared to over one hundred degrees and continuous beads of sweat ran down our faces. We were tired and dehydrated with the sun beating down on our heads. I heard the starving babies crying for anything that would fill their stomachs. Children and adults alike were seeking places to find shelter from the heat and humidity.

Our family huddled together and slept on the side of the road for several nights. Shortly after the sunrise on the morning of May 28, 1975, we prepared our belongings and walked slowly with thousands of Hmong to the Hin Heup Bridge. When we approached the bridge, we abruptly stop-ed in our tracks. Numerous people with sunken eyes of fear were running towards us screaming and crying. A gentleman grabbed my father's arm and shouted, "People are being threatened by soldiers up front and if anyone crosses the bridge they will be shot and killed." In terror, my father commanded us to stay low, and we waited. About five minutes later, we heard the thundering noises of gun shots being fired, resonating in the air. It was catastrophic, chaotic and unbelievable. The innocent were running, screaming in agony as they hurried our way. There were several wounded men, women, and children being carried by their families, dripping with the crimson blood that left messy stains upon the dirt road. My father told everyone to retreat immediately! We gathered our things and ran as fast as we could to the truck where we had parked it. My uncle drove us back to Vang Vieng. There was fear in our eyes and exhaustion filled the atmosphere, but we were safe and providentially no one in our family was hurt. As we drove away from the Hin Heup Bridge, my father found an old abandoned house about ten miles up the road, and we took refuge for the night. My father took the night watch to make sure we were safe. I sat next to him, puzzled by his silence but I could sense the despair and the uncertainty of what could become of us.

I woke up to my father and the men in the group discussing the next plan of action. We needed to cross the Mekong River in order to get to Thailand. In order to achieve this, we had to get traveling permits. My father left that afternoon and returned with three traveling permits for Vientiane, the capital of Laos. My father, my older brother, and I took a taxi cab to Vientiane the following day. Along the way we encountered many military check points and every time we stopped, I would hold my breath and peek out the window to make sure my father was safe. Once we arrived in Vientiane, my father went directly to the Laos Consulate and filed for several traveling permits for the rest of the families. It was not easy to obtain the permits. My father sought out every possible means by using his military and police affiliations to acquire the permits, going so far as bribing the officers with hundreds and thousands of Lao kip

(Laos's currency). After the traveling permits were filed, we had to wait a whole month before we could obtain them. During the entire, long wait, we were homeless in the city of official corruption and lived with the constant fear of being captured and shot. After thirty days elapsed, we were able to get over thirty permits, enough for everyone. We left early the next morning to retrieve the permits.

On the return trip from Vientiane to Vang Vieng, our taxicab sped too quickly and the car lost control around a narrow curve. Our vehicle rolled over several times down a steep hill and I could see my life flashing before my eyes. Everyone screamed and before we knew it, we had landed in a ditch. It happened so quickly and we were all silent when my father asked if everyone was alright. I nodded my head when our eyes met for the very first time. I promptly shifted my gaze towards his arm and I could see the trembling in his hands. My brother and I sustained minor cuts and bruises to our faces and arms, but thankfully, by God's grace, we survived the accident.

As we prepared for our long journey to Thailand, my father made arrangements for our transportation. He gathered the remainder of our savings, sold the spare traveling permits along with his motorcycle, and paid 900,000 Lao kip to trustworthy locals to guide us across the Mekong River Bank to Thailand. A few days later, we gathered our belongings and got into my uncle's truck and cautiously made our way to Vientiane with the whole family. When we arrived, we spent a nerve wracking night in an old abandoned house made of cement, covered with aluminum sheeting.

My father discovered that some of our relatives in the city also wanted to flee to Thailand. Because of his benevolent heart, he invited them to join our family in the pursuit of freedom. That day there were more than seventy of us crowded into a small, abandoned house impatiently waiting for the next step of action.

My father whispered to everyone, "We must be silent and sleep during the daytime, and then be ready to walk several miles to the Mekong River bank tonight."

The tiny house was hot and humid, and we were sweating excessively, exhausted from traveling in the heat. It had been days since we had showered and I could not remember the last time we had anything to eat. We could have been querulous but it was essential to stay silent because the communist guards patrolled the location every so often. If our enemies found us, all of us would be captured and shot instantly!

As the sun bid us farewell and the stars and the moonlight illuminated the earth's surface, all seventy of us, children and adults, quietly gathered our belongings. With my sister strapped tightly onto my mother's chest, a few pots and pans, and the clothing on our backs we were prepared for the unknown journey ahead of us. Led by my father and the guide, we fearfully walked those few, but seemingly long miles to the Mekong River. The crickets chirped all around us as we walked in darkness. We were afraid and grew weary. The dirt caked our feet and I began to see shadows lurking beyond the wilted trees. With every last hope and bit of strength in us, we finally approached the riverbank. We could see the motor canoes that were waiting to take us across the Mekong River to Thailand. We stepped quietly into the canoes and then all the engines turned on at once. As the canoes sped quickly across the river, water splashed against the side of the canoe, leaving tiny droplets against my skin. My reflection was a mere silhouette within the Mekong River so I couldn't see my hope filled eyes and trifle smirk. Within minutes we were on the other side on the river in a totally different and strange country. There were several Thai men that had spotted our canoes and waited for us on shore. As we got out of the canoes, the men approached my father with guns and demanded money.

"We're being robbed!" exclaimed my grand uncle.

My father and uncles quarreled with the Thai men for an extended period of time. Coincidentally, Thai police officers arrived. The Thai men quickly disappeared into the bushes and we were so thankful no one was hurt. The Thai police officers called for two large trucks and we loaded our belongings in as fast as we could. We got into the trucks and took a bumpy ride to the local temporary refugee camp. We settled there for three days and then took another long ride to the Nong Khai Refugee Camp, where our lives were safe....for now.

Life in the Nong Khai Refugee Camp, Thailand

We arrived at Nong Khai Refugee Camp on a hot, sunny summer day. The camp was surrounded with iron military wires, and the air was filled with amber dust, still thick with hanging dew. There were long buildings made with bamboo poles, topped with aluminum sheets. Each of the buildings was divided into ten family compartments, where ten to fifteen people found ways to live in the small, unsanitary spaces.

Life in the refugee camp was not what we had expected. Thousands of Hmong refugees had resettled in the compound before we arrived. I saw smoke rising from each building as women prepared food for their families. Babies were crying and children were playing in the dirt roads with their wooden spinning tops. Our group of seventy carried our belongings into the camp across the narrow beaten pathways to the registration headquarters. As we approached the building, we waited in silence and confusion. A man opened the door and asked who the leader of our group was. My father swallowed his fear, stepped forward, and waved his hand backwards, halting us as he walked into the building alone. We waited anxiously for him to come out unharmed. After more than thirty agonizing minutes, my father finally came outside and informed us that all of the building compartments were occupied and that there was no more room for us. If we wanted to stay, we would have to wait until the new buildings were built.

"But how long do we have to wait?" someone asked.

My father replied that it could be a few weeks or even a whole month.

Everyone was whispering, "How are we going to live?"

Just when we were so close to living again, we had to face this awful predicament standing in our path.

My father told everyone that he would find a temporary place for us within the refugee camp. We stood and waited as he explored the campsite. Half an hour later, he came back and told everyone that he had found a place where we could settle for the time being, while awaiting the completion of the new buildings.

"Follow me!" he said.

We picked up our belongings and followed him to an open dirt field within the camp. My father, grandfather, and uncles searched for wood, gathered countless wooden poles, metal poles, and metal sheets that were strewn upon the ground. They brought back what they could salvage, and built several small huts that housed all of us. Because the huts were insufficiently built, we felt the breeze blowing through the sheet walls from one end of the hut to the other. During the daytime, as the sun blazed down from the cloudless, sapphire sky the breeze always felt nice, drying and cooling the sweat away from my face. But at night, that same breeze felt chilly, and I could see the goose bumps forming on my skin. Whenever it rained, we crowded ourselves into the middle of the hut to avoid getting wet. We would sit huddled together, watching the raindrops bounce in the dirt. Food was scarce. Daily we were told not to waste any food, not even the smallest scrap. We were given food and water supplies once each week, but it was never enough to feed the entire family. My mother caught rainwater in a bucket so that we could use it for cooking whenever we ran out of water. We rarely washed ourselves or took showers unless it rained.

We waited impatiently for a month until the new buildings were completed and we were able to move in. My father was made chief of the building because of his strong leadership skills and his former rank as a police captain.

My Brother, My Inspiration

My older brother, Pao, was my biggest role model. Despite the struggle and the hunger to live and survive, he was and still is my greatest hero. Although he was only 9 years old, Pao risked his life every day to bring food home for us to eat. Because food was always limited in the camp, he would wake up before sunrise, and sneak out of the camp to fish and catch frogs along the small stream nearby to feed my sister and me. One morning I caught Pao right before he left.

He looked at me and said, "Be good, I will be back and I will bring you the biggest fish you will ever eat."

I smiled, quickly closed my eyes and went back to sleep as he disappeared into the dark. One day, Pao came home and became very ill. He had a high fever, chest congestion with a persistent cough, and chills with shivering. As his illness worsened, he would grunt with his ribs retracted as he gasped for air. Pao was having difficulty breathing and there was nothing I could do to help him. I would sit at the end of his bed and wait for him to speak, move or do something. My parents were devastated and did everything in their power to help him, using all of the traditional Hmong treatments—praying, needle pricking, pinching the nasal bridge, massaging, cupping and giving herbal remedies—but there was no improvement. His condition deteriorated quickly. As the last resort, my parents took my brother to the refugee health center, where they were told that nothing could be done.

My parents decided they would try to get him to a real hospital, a Thai hospital, outside of the refugee camp. My father had to go through many obstacles and filled out many forms in order to be cleared by the local officials to leave the camp ground. After waiting for enervating hours, my brother became even more seriously ill and was suffocating. Finally, because of my brother's critical condition, we were cleared by the officials to leave the campground to go to the nearest hospital, thirty minutes away by car. My parents were jobless and had no money for the transportation. They had to borrow money from our relatives with the promise of paying them back when they returned.

My father was able to get a taxi, so we transported my brother to the nearest Thai hospital. I could not leave my brother's side and begged my father to allow me to go with them. As we rode down the bumpy roads, I could see my brother's chest uncontrollably rising and falling. His ribs were retracting, and I could see them through his thin white t-shirt. He was gasping for air and moaning, clutching his pain stricken chest. Finally, we arrived at the hospital, but there was no one to greet us or to bring a wheelchair to transport my brother. My father quickly carried my brother in his arms into the emergency room.

Once we were inside, a nurse came and told my father to place my brother on one of the stretchers near the window. We waited for hours, watching him struggle to breathe. Still, no one did anything as he lay there fighting for his life. It seemed like forever before anyone came over to speak to us.

When the words finally came after the long, excruciating, wait, they were unbearable to hear, "There is nothing we can do."

They lacked the decency to even examine my brother! The tears in my eyes blurred my vision and I could barely breathe. I began to pant. I grabbed my brother's hands and begged God to save him. I had a sudden realization that all of the doctors at the hospital had a chance to help my brother. They had all the credentials, the tools, the medicines, and the ability to save him, but they forgot about their humanity. A doctor should be able to empathize with the suffering and use their gifts to help everyone. Suddenly, my body felt numb and my heart palpitated through my chest wall as I looked into my brothers eyes; I could see him giving up. I grasped onto his hands tightly until I could feel the sweat building up as we held onto each other. His grip began to loosen and I finally spoke.

I took an oath with my brother, Pao, that one day, "I will become a doctor and heal the hearts of others. I will do my very best to save anyone who needs medical care without hesitation."

It was an oath and a dream that was seemingly impossible, but I kept it deep in my heart.

As we watched my brother's last gasp for air, his eyelids went limp and his desperate attempts to breathe came to an end. My mother cried out for help. One of the nurses arrived and carelessly pronounced my brother dead. I watched my mother's tears run down her face as she mourned for the loss of her son. At first she cried loudly, but then she grew numb and speechless. My father pulled her out of the emergency room and helped her sit down on a chair. He tried to hold back his pain, clenching his teeth, but tears ran silently down his face. He had done everything he could to save my brother, but in the end my brother could not overcome his illness. My father wrapped Pao in an old white bed sheet and carried him back to the refugee camp.

Traditionally, when someone passed away, a proper burial ceremony would be performed with the thudding of drums, sending the spirit away, and the body would be placed in a closed casket. We were poor and had no money to give him a proper burial ceremony. Pao was wrapped in a blanket and placed underneath the rocky soil outside the refugee camp. My mother held much guilt for many months because she did not give him a proper burial. Unable to resign herself to it, she became depressed. Several months later, we discovered that my brother's grave was dug out, along with other graves, to expand the living space for other refugees to settle.

The suffering of being refugees continued for months. The agony of the mourning and the thundering sounds of the death drum continued to resonate day after day, night after night. Death for us was approaching.

Eventually my father finally said, "We are no longer safe here. We have to move on and leave this horrible place."

Towards the end of 1975, my father managed to hire two big trucks and smuggle us out of the Nong Khai Refugee Camp. We traveled many hours to get to another refugee camp, called Ban Vinai.

Life in Ban Vinai Refugee Camp, Thailand

The Ban Vinai Refugee Camp was located in the northeast part of Thailand, about fifteen miles from the Mekong River. It was a bigger camp that hosted thousands more refugees than Nong Khai Refugee Camp. There were two entry points—the East Wing and West Wing. Upon arrival in the new camp, we were able to receive an official family number and settled in Group 1, Camp 3, Building 8, and Compartment 8. The building had plywood walls, corrugateed aluminum sheet roofing, and ten compartments, each of which housed ten to fifteen family members. Adjacent to the west side of the building were smaller kitchen houses made with wooden poles, bamboo walls, and thatched roofs, one for each family to do their own cooking and dining.

I was about seven years old when we arrived at the new camp. Life was slightly better because there was more space for everyone. The influx of new refugees continued and my father invited more people to house in our building. There were more than one hundred and fifty people, with over seventy-five children who ranged in age from newborn to eighteen years old. Although we were uncertain of our future, the environment at the new refugee camp was more uplifting. I would play with kids my age around the buildings. We played with wooden spinning tops and played hide and seek games. Soccer was a passion for me. My friends and I formed a soccer team, and we kicked the plastic soccer ball with our naked feet. I became the captain of our team, and we won almost every game! I was known as one of the fastest runners and the best ball controller among the children. We competed with other teams of the same age for rubber bands and soccer balls.

One time we played soccer against the Laotian children who were taller and bigger than we were. I loved to play center forward position. I scored one or two goals within five minutes. We were proud that we scored first, but we made the other team angry, and they started to play violently. One of my teammates was seriously hurt during the game and a dispute broke out. The argument escalated into a huge fist fight. We won the game, but we lost the fight, and I sustained a black eye as did some of my teammates.

When I got home that evening, my father saw my black eye and he was furious. He chopped my soccer ball into little pieces with a knife and demanded that I eat the plastic bits. Luckily, he didn't force the plastic pieces down my throat. He did, however, tell me that if he ever caught me playing soccer again, he would beat me up and make me swallow the whole soccer ball. He whacked my legs and butt several times with a bamboo stick and then told me to kneel down on my knees for an entire hour. I broke down in tears and began to feel pain everywhere. I didn't understand why he was so rough on me. I just wanted to be like the other kids and play soccer. Later that night, my mother told me that my father was upset and disciplined me because he was worried and didn't want anything bad to happen to me. She told me he loved me very much and wanted me to study hard instead of playing soccer and getting hurt. Unfortunately, at that age I felt horrible when I almost lost my soccer team because of my father's concerns and love for me. He wanted me to grow up as a normal educated son.

However, despite the brutal punishment, I still disobeyed him and found ways to sneak out of our building to play soccer with my teammates. Soccer was my passion and I was not prepared to give it all up. I would ask my teammates to watch out for my father, and then I would run or hide if someone spotted him close by. I practiced soccer several times a day and played at least one game against another team each day before sunset. I thought soccer was a good way to keep me out of trouble but instead I ended up in more fights and made new enemies. These did not, however, stop me from playing soccer.

I was passionate about watching movies that played in the refugee camp. Once a month the Thai movie industry would come in and showed new Thai, Chinese and American movies. My cousins, Tou, Bee, Boun, Chue, and I were movie fanatics! We would do anything to earn coins, so that we could watch all the movies. We harvested watermelon, cucumbers, bananas, papayas, and cabbage to sell along the street market to earn money. We would push candy carts around the camp all day long just to earn two baths (equal to ten cents in the U.S.). We watched almost all the Thai, Chinese, and American movies that were made from 1976 to 1979. Our favorite famous Thai actors were Sombat Metanee, Saraphong Chatree, Krung Srivilai and Dam Datsakorn. One of the most beautiful and memorable Thai actresses at the time was Ms. Naowarat Yuktanan. The most famous Chinese actors were Wang Yu, Bruce Lee and Jackie Chan. The most famous American actor was Steve McQueen, with the movie *The Great Escape*. Those movies inspired us to dream of new adventures and gave us a new perspective of life outside the refugee camp.

In 1976, I was enrolled in the second grade and started to learn the Thai language. Thai school regulations were very strict. We had to wear a uniform—a white short sleeve shirt and light brown shorts. My father had to work many long hours as a barber to earn enough money just to buy one uniform so that I could attend school like the other children.

He would always tell me: "Son, education is the key to becoming a successful person. Go to school and study hard."

My grand-uncle, Chang Ger Xiong, always prompted me to go to school and reminded me that education is the key to the future. These words echoed in my ears for the longest time.

Learning a new language was not easy for me or for the

other children. In order to succeed, I had to discipline myself to always attend class and spend many hours repeating and memorizing what I learned each day. Within six months, I was fluent in speaking, reading, and writing in Thai. Life in the refugee camp became easier in terms of communication.

The Drum of Agony

Roughly forty thousand Hmong refugees were crammed into the Ban Vinai Refugee Camp in 1979. Poor sanitation, malnutrition, and pandemic infectious diseases became the root of death. The Drum of Agony never stopped pounding. I called it "The Drum of Agony" because it was a major part of our traditional funeral setting, and represented the agony felt by those who had lost a loved one. The drum pounded for three days and three nights straight, or sometimes, even for seven days and seven nights, depending on whether the deceased was a young person or an elderly individual. The sound of the drum varied from three slow beats, to a smooth beat, then a soft beat to various fast beats, loud beats, or thunderous beats. To little children, the sound of the drum was very terrifying, but after four years of living in the camp and being exposed to so many deaths, our minds became immune to the sound.

What petrified us most came after the drumming, the ghosts of the lingering dead with unfinished business. One night, my friends and I were playing hide and seek in what we called our yard. We had a close friend who lived up the hill who also played with us that night. As the game started, she was partnered up with me and followed me wherever I hid. Her long black hair touched her shoulders and she wore a beautiful, long white dress, which was sort of unusual for that night. She didn't say a word, but she would smile at me from time to time. The seekers did not find us and we won the game that night.

The next morning her parents came to our house and told my parents that their daughter had drowned the morning before. I could not believe what I heard.

I told her parents, "She was playing hide and seek with us last night."

Her parents replied, "No, she went fishing with her brothers' yesterday morning. Then she swam—somehow she drowned. We found her body this morning."

Her mother then wailed, continuing to mourn her death. I felt sad, and we all mourned for her, but at the same time I was terrified and frightened. Her funeral was held for three days with the sound of the pounding drum, and qeej—a free reed musical instrument that consists of seven bamboo pipes attached to a wooden wind chamber which is used to communicate with the spirit world. That was the last time I saw her.

A few months later, my younger sister became ill with chickenpox. She developed a blistering rash all over her body and was burning up with fever. She laid in bed, tossing and turning, racked with intractable pain. My parents took her to the refugee hospital and were told that it was too late to do anything. She developed sepsis and within twenty-four hours my sister Phoua took her last breath and went to live with the Lord. With the second death in my family, I became more tenacious in becoming a doctor, in the hope of saving lives. My dream of becoming a medical doctor and my vision of saving people was still seemingly impossible, but I kept it in my heart.

The Immigration Process

During the month of November of 1979, the Ban Vinai Refugee Camp became enormously congested with the uncontrollable influx of refugees. There were so many newcomers that life seemed almost impossible. Infectious diseases escalated, and the Drum of Agony continued to pound day and night. After four years in the camp, my parents were fed up with the political corruption and decided it was time to leave and begin a new life in another country. Immigration lines continued to be opened to the United States, France, Bolivia, and Australia. Fortunately, our decision was not a difficult one to make. My grandfather and uncle had emigrated to the U.S. a few years earlier and wanted us to follow them to America. My parents started the immigration process by filling out numerous forms and the immigration agency had to verify that our grandfather and uncle in California would sponsor us.

Four weeks after we submitted our immigration forms, Mr. Jerry Daniels called us for an interview. He assigned an immigration number that began with the letter T, followed by five numbers (T45960). During the interview, my parents were asked the same questions that were asked of all refugees who wanted to come to America—what did you do in Laos? Do you have another name? Is this your wife? Are these your children? Why do you want to go to America? What is your relationship to your sponsors? Does anyone in your family have any chronic diseases or infectious diseases, such as tuberculosis or lung cancer? Is anyone terminally ill? One of the most popular responses to why the Hmong wanted to immigrate to the United States was, "We follow our leader—General Vang Pao, to America."

About a month later, we were granted permission to go to America. We were each given a complete physical exam, immunizations, and a chest X-ray to rule out contagious diseases such as tuberculosis and terminal lung cancer. The physical exam included a very thorough head to toe analysis. We were not used to having our breasts or genitals examined by strangers, so we were very hesitant and uncomfortable, but did as we were told. Otherwise, we would not be approved by the immigration officers to go to America. We chuckled at the same time, trying to overcome our fears and embarrassment. Thankfully, our physical exam results were normal, our chest x-rays were negative for any acute or chronic lung diseases, and our immunizations were all up to date. We were told that we had passed the examination and needed to wait for our names to be announced for the exact date and time of departure. We were excited and hopeful that we would finally get another opportunity to live in the land of the free—America.

We waited anxiously and started giving away all our

possessions to our relatives. We kept only necessary and valuable items. After one long month of waiting, our names were finally announced among one hundred other Hmong refugees that would go to America on February 8, 1980.

CHAPTER THREE

Journey to the United States of America

Leaving Ban Vinai Refugee Camp

When the departure date was finally announced, we rejoiced and excitement filled the atmosphere! As the date drew near, we became more anxious about the new world awaiting us. Where would we live? Are the people there kind? How could we start our lives the right way? What language do they speak? How would we communicate with them? My parents did not sleep for days and every day they remind all of the neighbors, "We are going to America."

We were told to always be prepared and to expect the buses to arrive anytime on February 8, 1980. When the date finally came, we hauled our belongings and waited on an open dirt field. There were children, parents, relatives, and friends of all ages awaiting the journey to a new life. I rested my cloth bag on the dusty ground and planted myself next to my parents and my siblings. We waited for what seemed to be an eternity and suddenly, from a far distance, we saw three small objects approaching us.

People shouted, "They're here! They're here to take us to America!"

The buses slowly advanced onto the dirt field and everyone started to gather their things. We waited impatiently until our names were called. The relatives who followed behind to bid us goodbye grew tearful and we all began to cry, partially because we did not want to leave them behind and because of the emotional strain.

We had suffered so much and the long wait to freedom was finally here! But could we trust the Americans? We were told that it would be The Land of Opportunity, but how could we be so sure? What if these buses took us somewhere totally unexpected? What if there were soldiers who would put us in prison? After all, it wasn't unheard of; it had happened to many other Hmong families after the war. Some of them had simply disappeared, or their corpses were found lying on the side road or in the jungle. The very thought made me shiver.

And yet, we were still excited! How could we not be? The desperate wait had filled our minds and hearts with so many hopes and dreams!

But now that the buses had arrived, it was time to say goodbye to our families and friends. If anything should happen to us, this would be the last time that we would see each other.

We climbed into the bus with tears running down our faces. There was a mixture of sadness, fear and happiness all at the same time! We boarded; then the buses started to slowly move and we were on our way. Our stomachs churned as we looked out the windows and saw our relatives and friends running after us, clinging to the sides of the bus because they did not want us to leave. After a short while, the buses accelerated and they were no longer able to hold on.

A Place to Rest

After riding in the bus for many hours, we finally pulled up to a metal barred gate. We had no idea what was going on or where we were. Everyone began to panic and fear spread like a virus. Eventually, someone informed us that this was a rest stop and that we had to wait for the next bus that would take us to Bangkok. After three or more hours had gone by, we grew weary and concerned. Only God knew what was going to happen next.

We were directed to join the other families on the concrete slab in the middle of an open field. We were given a nylon sheet and were told to build a tent, to shelter and protect us from mosquitoes for the night. There were no beds, blankets or pillows. We slept on the cold cement floor with a single light bulb hanging above our heads. Luckily for us, we had some relatives with the same last name—Xiong— who stayed with us and we were able to get a few supplies from them. We huddled close together on the hard cement floor, but it was difficult to sleep even though we were so exhausted. We were hungry, dehydrated and our lips were cracked, but we endured the night.

We shivered because in February, the mountains froze, sending the cold breeze at night. The towering walls around the camp blocked some of the wind but we could still feel the draft brushing against our skin as a breeze made it over. We trembled because every now and then a huge rat came running across the concrete slab! Sometimes the rat took a quick glance at us with its big red eyes. I guess the rats were hungry, too, looking for any scraps they could find. But we had no scraps for them, let alone for ourselves. It occurred to my sisters and me that if we could catch the rats we could build a little fire and have something to eat. However, the thought of the big rat scared me, overpowering my hunger.

In the morning, there was a lot of commotion about where we were. There was a very tall wall that surrounded the place, and we could hear people inside coughing, crying in pain, and moaning. We discovered there were many opiate addicts who were being held in the camp for detoxification along with those who had tuberculosis. They were kept there until they died or became well enough to leave. Neither addicts nor sick people were allowed to go to the United States, which meant that some of the people there would have to wait six months or more before they could ever see beyond the walls. My family was in good health and was kept far away from the sick.

From the time we arrived and settled, we survived on water grass soup and whatever we could find. We were excited when we found out that we would be given some rice and a few vegetables, sea cress, and cabbage, to eat. The rice tasted like heaven because we were so hungry! We were given food again that night, more rice and cabbage. We sat there eating together as day turned into night. We could not see the moon or the stars because the metal sheets obscured our view and the high walls imprisoned us. However, we were blessed that our family was safe and healthy.

At this time, I was eleven years old. Every day my parents would tell me, "Get up early and go to the immigration office to check if our names appear on the list to go to America."

I made it my responsibility to check the list every morning. After two long days of waiting, a gentleman from the office arrived in our area with a white sheet of paper. Everyone ran like crazy towards him, similarly to a crowd getting out of control for free giveaways. So I ran with them, jostling against the crowd, holding my breath as the man from the office took his little hammer and tap, tap, tap, nailed the sheet of paper to the wall. When I got close enough, I pressed my nose against the paper and traced my finger down the list until I saw them—our names!

I jumped for joy and said, "Okay! We're going to America!"

Once I got a grip of myself, I raced home and shouted to my parents, "Get up, get up, our names are on the list, we're going to American Land!"

We quickly packed our things and headed out the door. Some people saw us and began to laugh as we hustled towards the immigration office.

One of them said, laughing again, "You're not leaving until tomorrow morning!"

I said, "But we already packed everything!"

And they said, "Well, you will just have to wait."

We walked back to our tent in embarrassment but we

held onto the thought of going to America the following morning.

When the time came, there were closed to twenty people who had already boarded, but there was still enough room for all of us. We anxiously waited for each of our names to be called and then one by one, we took the last few steps from the campground onto the bus. I sat next to my mother. She looked tense as if she had forgotten something, but I knew we could not go back anymore. We were leaving our old lives behind and moving to an unknown land to start over.

The bus ride was a very long one. The roads were poorly paved with dirt and rocks. It wasn't until night fall that we reached the airport. It was dark and we had just been jostled around enough to awaken our tired little bones.

A Long Flight to Freedom

At the airport, there were cars and flashing lights everywhere. We could hear airplanes flying above our heads. The bus came to a stop on the concrete road and we were directed to take our belongings and exit the bus. We walked single-file through a door and proceeded to check-in. When we approached the ticketing counter we were asked to submit our immigration papers. After they reviewed our immigration papers and stamped them with the seal of approval, we sat and waited to for our plane.

The morning came quickly and one of the Thai immigration officers came over and informed us to get ready. We walked through a long hallway to reach our gate. Once we arrived, one of the officers double checked our immigration papers and issued our boarding passes. He told us to wait until we were called to board the airplane. Walking through the corridor, I saw a gigantic airplane with "PAN AM" written on it in big blue letters. PAN AM (Pan American) was the principal and largest international air carrier in the United States at the time. I had never been on an airplane before and prior to departure, butterflies filled my stomach.

We stopped in Hong Kong to refuel the airplane and by then we were all hungry. My mother said, "Don't eat anything they give you!"

They were not sure what these strangers would give us, or if the food was safe to eat. So after a few minutes, the stewardess came and brought each one of us an unfamiliar round red fruit that we had never seen before. Immediately, my mother said, "No! Don't eat it!"

We had never seen a fruit like that before—big, round, and red. We studied it very closely, but no matter how hungry we were, we did not eat the fruit—apples.

There were different kinds of people on our plane. Although there had been a few Americans in Long Cheng, and Americans that came to the refugee camp, we were not used to seeing so many. There were people of different colors and ethnicities, and we tried our best to not speak or make eye contact. It was frightening and fascinating at the same time.

We landed in San Francisco the next day. We were tired and hungry. We proceeded through the immigration process, and by the time we got to the hotel, it was already 9 o'clock at night. When we arrived in our hotel room, there were two huge beds that felt like clouds when we laid on them. Through further exploration I discovered another person in our hotel bathroom. His eyes were sunken in and his cheekbones protruded like daggers. His belly button bulged out of hunger but his stomach concaved below his piano-like rib cage. Overall he looked very thin and malnourished. As I tried to touch him, he mimicked my movements. Surprised, I jumped back, in shock of my own reflection in the mirror.

With no money and little knowledge of the new land, we went to bed hungry that night. Our hunger was moderated by the beautiful view from our hotel window. Colorful lights radiated through the city of San Francisco. We sat quietly and watched the flashing lights and listened to the sounds of cars and people speaking in a strange language.

The next morning, a bus came to pick us up and we boarded another flight to Orange County, California. As our plane approached Orange County, I looked out the window and saw many cars and tall buildings everywhere. I was amazed at how tiny everything was and could not wait for the plane to land. Finally our plan landed.

As I stepped out of the plane I said, "Wow, this is like heaven."

My uncle and aunt were waiting for us outside the gate. It was a Kodak moment without a camera. As we walked to my uncle's car I spotted a tall bronze statue of a man who wore a cowboy hat and a revolver on the right side of his hip. I looked into his eyes and touched him. I asked him to grant me the privilege to fulfill my dreams.

My uncle told me, "That's John Wayne. He is a famous cowboy actor."

We all scrunched into my uncle's Toyota Corolla station wagon, but that did not matter. We were reunited with grandpa, grandma, and the rest of the family. The house had three bedrooms and a sunroom in the back yard. It didn't matter that there were thirty-five or forty people living in the same house; we were safe, together once again, and we had a place to call home. We made it to America, and we knew our lives would change for the better.

There were, of course, many obstacles to overcome. We did not speak English and it was very difficult to transition into the American way. We were taught to say yes more than no just to be polite and kind.

There were times when I walked down the street and people would come up to me and say, "Can I spit on you?"

I didn't understand what they were saying so I would respond, "Yes, yes."

Then they would spit on me. Other times people would ask me, "Can we kick you?"

And I would reply, "Yes, yes!" And I would be kicked and beaten up. I had much to learn.

CHAPTER FOUR

My New Life in America

Our First Home in America

After living with my grandparents, uncles, aunt, and cousins in Santa Ana, California for a month, we found an apartment on the east side of the city. I imagined our new home to be huge, with 5 bedrooms, many beautiful cookie cutter win-dows and a white picket fence. We all shared one bedroom at my grandparent's house, so moving our belongings was not difficult.

My uncle said, "It's going to take us fifteen minutes to get there."

We used my Uncle Nao Tou's Toyota Corolla station wagon to haul everything to the new home. I wanted to be cool like my cousins so I hopped in the back trunk with them. I did not know that this was illegal and unsafe, but I learned the hard way when we got into a car accident. Because of all the talking and distractions, my uncle rear-ended the car ahead of us.

He quickly shouted, "Everyone get out of the car, before the police get here!"

Thankfully, we did not get a ticket and finally, we

reached the apartment. We parked our car along the street and walked through the gates. It was nothing like I had envisioned. It reminded me of being in captivity at the Ban Vinai Refugee Camp. There were many children running around on the playground with swings, spring metal horses, slides, and seesaws. Many of the children were Hmong, and this brought back flashbacks from the camp. Bad memories flushed in my mind with the echoing sound of the Drum of Agony. There was a swimming pool near the center of the apartment complex where adults and children were swimming and splashing water. It reminded me of the big pond in the Bai Vinai Refugee Camp where I used to swim and children drowned. My uncle told us that there were several Hmong families living in the apartment complex, and that it would be nice to have them as our neighbors to keep us safe.

He also said, "I was able to get an apartment for your family next to a Hmong Moua Clan family."

We met the Moua family and discovered they had a son who was the same age as me. We spoke with the Moua family briefly and glanced through the apartment. It had two bedrooms in the upper floor, a small kitchen, and living room on the first floor. The manager told us to follow him to the clubhouse to sign the rental agreement contract. We were clueless about what we were signing. Back in Laos, we did not have paper contracts because we believed trustful bonds were better than written ones. Somehow, despite the language barrier, my mom managed to sign the rental agreement contract and we were given the key to our new apartment.

We went back to the apartment and opened the door, and my mom said, "This is our home now."

Shortly after we moved in, my mother and I got on a bus and took a long ride to the local welfare department on 17th Street in the City of Santa Ana. We were going to apply for government funding to help with our apartment rent, food stamps to pay for food, and health insurance to cover our medical bills in case we became ill. When we arrived at the welfare department there were a lot of people waiting in lines to be interviewed. We waited in line for an hour before we reached the receptionist's desk. As we approached the desk, the receptionist started to speak in English, and we had no clue what she was saying.

I started to speak to her in broken English, "Here...for money, money...money you know!"

I heard her say what sounded like "What's the name?"

I had my index finger pointed to my lips and responded, "Name...name, oh yes, yes, yes! My name is..Xa!

The lady said, "No, no, no...I mean your mother's name."

I responded, "Oh, mother's name...her name, Yer."

She asked, "May I have your I-94 and social security card?"

I responded, "I ninety-four...social-curity car. No car! I take bus!"

I could sense the lady's frustration and quickly turned to my mother. The lady reached over and took my mom's purse and started searching for my mom's I-94 and social security cards. Finally, she found the cards and registered my mom onto the registry.

She said, "You may have a seat and someone will call you for an interview."

Again, we had no idea what she was saying. I told my mom to sit but there was no chair in front of the receptionist desk so we kept standing with confusion.

I responded to the lady, "No chair here!"

She said, "Over there!" and pointed to a cluster of empty chairs in the corner.

I responded, "Oh...I see...chair!" We walked to the chairs in embarrassment and sat down. Everyone stared at as though we were aliens, visiting from another planet.

We waited for more than two hours. Finally, my mother's name was called by a Hmong lady. She was the social worker who was assigned to our case.

"Fortunately, she is Hmong," I whispered to my mother.

She took us into a tiny room for an interview. My mother answered a ton of questions while she completed the forms. We were very thankful that she helped us; otherwise we would not have been able to receive the appropriate funding.

When we finished at the welfare department, we took another long bus ride home. There were a lot of strange people on the bus who were looked intimidating, so we kept to ourselves. When we made it back home, I told my cousins about the big world and my experience on the bus. Every-one was amazed we made it back in once piece.

The First Shopping Center

We resided close to a shopping center called Standard Plaza. Since we did not have a car, my father bought me a bike to run errands and purchase food and supplies. We did most of our grocery shopping at Stater Brothers and bought clothing from the flea market. We received food stamps (paper money) from the government on a monthly basis, which was not real cash money. We could not use food stamps to buy supplies or personal clothing. One day I rode my bike to Stater Brothers and parked outside the store to buy a cabbage and a pack of ground beef. I came outside with my bag of food and my bike was gone. I asked around and no one admitted to seeing anyone taking my bike. I was in tears and terrified that my parents would scold me for losing my bike. I contemplated in my head what I would tell my parents but when I got home without my bike that evening, I burst into tears and my parents both knew what had happened.

My father said, "The bike is not important. You are more important and we are glad that you are not hurt."

I was relieved, but saddened that my new bike was long gone.

One time my father and I went to a local electronics store to buy parts for the broken radios and tape recorders at home. When we walked into the store, the salesmen began to make fun of us. They imitated what we said, giggling and mocking us. We knew what was going on, but we ignored them anyway. My father couldn't speak English, so he made hand gestures in hopes that the salesmen would understand. They started chuckling and chitchatting with one another, but we had no idea what they were uttering.

All we could understand was when they said, "No, No, No!"

I told my father that maybe they were trying to tell us that they did not have the parts we were looking for. We turned around and left the store. When we came home, I sat and thought about what occurred at the electronics store. The salesmen were rude and disrespectful because we could not speak English. This really upset me and motivated me to go to school and learn English.

Going to School

I was nervous to attend school in America, but I was excited to learn English so I could get a job to help my family. My sisters and I were enrolled at Theodore Roosevelt Elementary School in Santa Ana, California. I was enrolled in fourth grade and my sister attended second grade. The first few days of school were atrocious. Many students laughed at me when I attempted to speak English. They also pointed at me and called me *"poor Chino"* because I did not have nice matching clothes and wore blue rubber sandals. I was unaware that bullying was not tolerated in school so I endured getting spit on, mocked, and kicked around during recess. One day during class the teacher called my name to answer a question about a reading assignment. I did not understand her question. Some of the students started to laugh. I felt awkward so I rolled a pencil off my desk onto the floor. I went under my desk to pick up the pencil and never came back up. She walked over to my desk and said something to me, but I still had no idea what she was saying. I looked at her and felt embarrassed. My classmates were laughing as she pulled me from under the table and told me to sit in my chair. I went home that day and complained to my mother that learning English was hard and that I would never go back to school again.

My mother looked me in the eyes and said, "Education is created by humans and not by evil...it is learnable. You can and you will learn."

I listened to my mother's words of wisdom and wiped my tears immediately. I promised my mother to go back to school and study harder.

My classmates of course, continued to joke around with me, but I did not let them affect my learning capability. I spent many hours reading, writing, and pronouncing English words outside of school. I was pronouncing English words in my sleep. My mom started to worry that she might have turned me into a fanatic bookworm son. Within a month, I had finished the class curriculum and received a certificate for being the student of the month. From that time on, the students in my class began to notice me in a different light. They slowly stopped teasing me and going to school became more bearable.

A House across Town

A few months later, my parents found a house closer to my grandpa and uncles. The house was near Santa Ana Centennial Park on the mid-south side of Santa Ana. We moved to our new home on King Street. It had three bedrooms, a living room, a kitchen, a dining room, one full bath, and one half-bath. We even had a back yard and a front yard to ourselves this time. My father said the house would be safe for us to live in for the time being. There were six-feet-tall concrete walls in front of the house with two large locked gates. We felt like we were in prison, but we felt very safe when we were inside the gates.

We raised chickens, pigeons, and occasionally ducks. In the back yard, my mother planted herbs and vegetables: cabbage, radishes, onions, cilantro, sugar cane, squash, and mint. There was also a guava tree and an orange tree in the front yard. We didn't have to go to the store to buy vegetables—we could just pick them from the backyard.

Along with the move, I had to transfer to a new school—Diamond Elementary School on the west side. Assimilating to a new school was difficult because I had to make new friends again. English was still a struggle for me but math was very easy. I began to trade with my classmates by telling them that I would help them with their math homework if they helped me with English. My plan was a success and I even made some new friends. I graduated from Diamond Elementary School and went on to Carr Middle School across the street.

My Parents Receiving an Education

My father was a remarkable leader. My father had an immense heart and always wanted everyone to live in harmony. He was a man of integrity and valued everyone equally. He provided charitable services to all people without a selfish motive. He protected his family, his neighbors, and his people. He emptied his pocket change for those in need and never turned down an opportunity to help others. He opened our home to those who did not have shelter. On many occasions we had more than thirty-five people living in our house for several months at a time. When we cooked, we had to cook rice in two large rice cookers and fry two large cabbages with a few pounds of pork, beef, or fish. People would come to our house to live with us, and my father would support them until they were able to get back on their feet.

My father worked very hard repairing broken stereos and selling fish to the local neighbors. Eventually, he was able to save enough money to buy his first used car, a white Mercury Zephyr station wagon. My father would drive to the supermarket for groceries, take us to school, and pick us up every day. When a Hmong person passed away in our town, my father would donate to help with their funeral expenses. He went the extra mile to support his community despite being poor. In his heart, he longed for the happiness of others more than his own. My mother was very supportive of his choices and shared similar values.

My parents were encouraged to attend school for ESL

(English as a Second Language) courses. They would sit next to each other along with their friends, and if the teacher asked a question, everybody would pretend as though they didn't hear what the teacher said. Other times, the teacher would ask a question and my father, my mother and the rest of their friends would look at each other and wait to see who would answer first.

If one person said yes, the rest of them would nod their heads and say, "Yes, Yes, Yes!"

But the teacher would say, "No, No, No!"

Then everyone would say, "No, No, No!" and laughed.

The teacher taught them how to pronounce a certain word and my father, mother, and everyone would say, "Good! Good! Good!" applauding her accuracy. But the teacher would say, "No, that's not good!" And everyone would laugh again. When the teacher assigned homework, everybody would copy off of each other.

My father said, "Either we all get 100 percent or we all get zeros." Although they struggled with the English language, my parents managed to complete the course and utilized their English when it was needed.

After a while, my father began to miss his life back in Laos where he was acknowledged as a great leader. In the United States, he no longer held the authority as a captain in the police force. The language barrier and unemployment were major setbacks for him. However, he pretended to be comfortable and hid his feelings. I could sense the stress and the frustration he had, but there was nothing we could do to help him. Nevertheless, he worked very hard to support his family and the rest of his relatives and the Hmong people across the United States.

Driving for the First and the Last Time

The first and last time my mother ever drove was in 1984. We were all standing on the side of the concrete driveway, watching my father teach my mother how to drive for the very first time. They both were in the car outside of the garage with the garage door closed.

My father said, "Driving is easy. All you have to remember is that the right pedal is the gas and the left pedal is the break. So don't step on the gas pedal when you want to stop the car. You only step on the gas pedal when you want the car to move forward."

My mom said, "Okay...I got it"

My father told my mom to slowly back up the car. He asked her to step on the brake and shift the gear into R. Instead she shifted the gear to D and stepped on the gas pedal. The car jumped and went right through the garage door. We all watched the garage fall apart, and we all glanced at each other and said, "Oh no! The garage is broken!" She never tried to drive again. From that experience, we realized that driving was not for everyone.

Life Changing

Summer went by quickly and fall arrived. I attended Carr Intermediate School, where I started as a sixth grader. I began making friends and picked up on soccer again, even with my father's disapproval. My friends and I quickly formed a soccer team. We called our team "Turbo." We practiced on the weekends and played against other teams during school tournaments. School continued to be a challenge, but I tried my best to survive. Each year I ended up with a B average, with occasional A's on my report card.

I had many male friends but shied away from girls. I was uncomfortable talking to girls because of the scar on my left chin. When I was about five years old, back in Laos, I tripped and fell. I jammed my face into a bamboo tree and cut my left chin. Luckily, the bamboo stick did not pierce through my mouth. My left chin was badly lacerated, and I was taken to the local clinic in Long Cheng, where stitches were sewn with unsterilized silk. My mother said that the wound became severely infected with bacteria and I almost died from the infection. Fortunately I survived but the scar remained. Because of this, I had a hard time interacting with people when I conversed. I would always avoid long conversations. I felt disfigured, almost monstrous. I had several friends who encouraged me, saying that I was handsome, smart, intelligent, and bright. But I wasn't sure if they truly meant it or if they just trying to be friends. Sometimes I would decline party invitations from my friends because I did not have the confidence to show my face.

Beauty Lies within the Heart

One day I had the opportunity to spend time alone

with my father. We went on a hunting trip at Big Bear Lake, California. We spent many hours together, and my father taught me everything I needed to know in order to survive in the real world.

He said to me, "Son, you can do anything you want. You can be anyone if you put your heart into it."

I decided to share my negative feeling about the scar on my left chin and what a great effect it had on my appearance and confidence.

He looked me in the eye and said, "Son, you are no different from the other kids. You are handsome, talented, and you even have a gift inside of you that no one else has. You can become anyone you wish to be."

He also said, "Don't be afraid to talk to girls. And if they don't want to talk to you, that's quite fine. One day you will find someone who will love you for who you are. You don't need to be scared of anyone. If they don't want to be your friend, that's okay. But remember one thing—study hard, become someone, and you will change things."

My father's words of encouragement embedded in my heart. I gained the confidence to be myself. I no longer saw the scar on my left chin. I felt great in the inside and looked great on the outside. I studied hard, did very well on each of my exams, and had many friends, including girls who wanted to study with me and get to know me. I learned that instinctively our minds are easily tuned to think negatively and label ourselves as being disabled or disfigured even though we are not. All we really need is someone to assure us that we are beautiful. As one of the greatest philosophers,

Plato, said, "Beauty lies in the eyes of beholder."

CHAPTER FIVE

Positive Inspiration

Life as a Teenager

Several years passed by and I began school at Valley High School in Santa Ana, California, with many of my friends. Within the Hmong community there was an uprising of gangsters, thieves, drug addicts, school truants and runaway delinquents. Because of all the negative activities, my parents established very strict rules in the family and enforced curfew hours for all the children.

My father said, "You go to school at 7:30 am and you come home right after school. Be home no later than 3:45 pm!"

If I was one minute late, my father would ask, "Why are you late?" I needed a good excuse to avoid consequences. Otherwise I would receive a very lengthy lecture. There was an enormous amount of pressure put on my shoulders because of my father's concerns. He wanted me to stay out of trouble and learn to make good decisions. He constantly reminded me that we were in a foreign country, and he needed to know where I was and whom I was with at all times. My father always encouraged me to choose my friends wisely and be with the right people. Being involved with the wrong people could bring problems.

After the long five days of school, I enjoyed my weekends the most. Sleeping in on a Saturday morning was ideal for any American teenager. My father, however, had a different set of goals. He loved to wake up around six o'clock in the morning, knock on our bedroom door and shout, "The sun has risen and the rooster has crowed. You must wake up."

My typical response to my father was, "Old man, don't you know that it's the weekend? I am tired. Please go away!"

Soon after my response, he pounded on the bedroom door several times and shouted even louder with still no response from me. The room grew silent for a split second while he raced to the garage and pulled out the lawn mower. He pushed the lawn mower back and forth, right outside my bedroom window until I woke up. On many occasions, I rushed out to the back yard in my pajamas, pleading for him to stop.

This was followed by his infamous lecture that began with, "If you wake up early, then you will get a broken spoon but if you wake up late then you will get a piece of a spoon."

This translated to, if you are awake early enough you will receive a spoon with a broken handle that will still allow you to scoop food, but if you wake up late, you will only receive a piece of the spoon that will not allow you to scoop food. Therefore you will start your day hungry. I always thought this was nonsense.

My father looked at the smirk on my face and said, "You will understand one day when you are my age."

In high school, I struggled with many of my classes. I did not know how to take notes nor study effectively. Our house was always filled with people, and it was just noisy in general. There was no such thing as peace in my home to effectively do homework or study. I would go to school early in the morning and finish my homework before my first class. If I had the time, I would glance through my homework a few minutes before exams.

My father was not a big fan of soccer during school, so, due to his strictness, I was not able to enroll in the high school soccer program with my friends. I found myself being left out of the crowd. On the weekends when my father was away, I would sneak out of the house to play soccer and practice back flips with my friends.

As a child growing up, I dreamed of becoming a famous soccer player. Every year I would watch the "Blue Thunder"—a Hmong soccer team played in the Hmong New Year Tournament in Fresno, California. They had the most skillful players of all the Hmong soccer teams in California. General Vang Pao's sons, nephews, and relatives brought the team together. They had discipline, leadership, and teamwork. The team won almost every tournament in California and they inspired me to practice hard in hopes that one day I could join them.

Because of my hard work and dedication, I had the opportunity to play on a different team. I was one of the speediest Hmong runners in Southern California at the time, so we named our team "Turbo." We played in many competitive tournaments and, although we weren't the most skillful team, we managed to win a few games here and there, placing in second or third place. I played many positions, including goalie, but my favorite was center forward, where I would always score points for my team.

As life went on, there was peer pressure to be accepted in social groups. I listened to my father, and chose my friends wisely. They were not the best in academics or sports, but they were decent acquaintances. We had similar thinking processes, good morals, and integrity. We also had common interests, kept ourselves busy, and stayed out of trouble.

High school was also the time to consider career choices and college options. My dream of becoming a medical doctor did not deviate after coming to America. I shared my dream with my friends but no one expressed any interest or support. They described my dream as either too difficult or too time consuming. Because of this, I kept this dream to myself. I envision the day I would slide my arms through the sleeves of my white coat and wrap my glistening stethoscope around the nape of my neck just like the young doctor Doogie Howser, MD on television. I would walk down the hospital hall and someone would page me, "Dr. Xiong, please come to the ER (Emergency Room)," or "Dr. Xiong, please come to the OR (Operating Room)," or "Dr. Xiong, please come to the ICU (Intensive Care Unit)." This vision imprinted in my mind and constantly reminded me to study hard and not abandon my dream of becoming a medical doctor.

Learning to Become a Leader

My father was a great leader, and everyone told me it was in my blood. I became an important member in the Lao Hmong Club at Santa Ana Valley High School. This particular club was developed to unify the Hmong students within our high school and to promote the Hmong culture and tradition. Attending meetings was an essential part of being a member. One day, I was sitting in the back of the room listening to the president of the club deliver his message. A light bulb went on and the thought, "I want to make a difference," came to me I said to myself, "I can make changes and lead this club in a more productive way to better serve the students." I visualized myself standing in front of the students, humbly speaking to them about self-improvement and giving back to the school and the community. I kept this vision to myself as I attended every meeting throughout my freshman, sophomore, and junior years. On the first week of my senior year—fall of 1985—the time had come to elect new officers to govern the club. The new election was held in one of the classrooms and the club members began to make nominations for the election. My name was spontaneously nominated among other members for the four positions: president, vice-president, secretary, and treasurer. The voting proceeded and the ballots were counted. Surprisingly, I had the most votes and was sworn in as President of the Lao Hmong Club for 1985-

1986. I expressed my vision to everyone, and with the support of my fellow officers and club members, we were able to fully reach our goals. We established an after school tutoring program for Hmong students who needed assistance with their studies. Hmong tradition and culture were demonstrated to educate other students. In addition to the tutoring program, the club also engaged in many fund raising events. One of the more popular events was the Thanksgiving Party. We were able to exceed our budget by selling candy bars and rewarded our members with a trip to Knott's Berry Farm.

During that same year, I also served as treasurer for the German Club and vice-president of the Student Government Club. Our student government club had the opportunity to join other high school clubs to take part in a political debate at the University of California Los Angeles (UCLA). Our debate team did not take the trophy that year, but it was one of the most intense verbal battles I had ever experienced. There was never a dull moment in high school; every day was filled with challenging activities and adventure.

A Rebellious Moment That Lead to an Inspiration

My friends and I planned to go to Disneyland two weeks before graduating from high school. It would celebrate our entire four years of high school together before we graduated, became adults and moved on with our lives. The day before our trip to Disneyland, I was excited because I anticipated driving my father's 1979 Mercury Zephyr station wagon without adult supervision.

The morning of the big day, when our rooster started to crow at 4 am, I jumped up from my bed and took a quick shower. I wore blue shorts and a clean, white polo shirt. My plan was to pick up my friends at 6 am. My father heard me getting ready to head out and immediately woke up. When I opened my bedroom door, I saw my father dressed up in a suit and tie standing in the middle of our living room.

He said, "You're not going anywhere today. You are going to go with me to a meeting."

I asked him, "What kind of meeting?" as a typical teen would have responded.

He answered, "Today, we will be having a meeting at ten o'clock, and I want you to accompany me to the meeting."

As any typical teenager, I responded, "But Dad, my friends and I have planned this trip for the whole year! This is the last time that we are going to spend time together. What are you trying to do?"

He said, "Son, you're not going. You are coming with me."

"Dad, come on," I complained. "This is the moment I've been waiting for! I'm going to be eighteen years old in August. Why are you doing this to me?"

My father said, "Son, don't question me. You must go with me to this meeting."

My arms tensed up and my entire body coiled, ready to explode. I was angry with my father.

I pounded the door snarling, "How could you possibly do this to me?"

My father didn't respond immediately.

He paused, and then said, "Someday you will understand."

I did not understand what he meant. There was nothing I could say or do but obey him with disappointment and anguish. I called my friends and told them the bad news.

My friends on the other end said, "Well, if you're not coming, then we'll just have to go without you" Some friends they were.

My father and I had breakfast together at our dining table. I didn't say a word to him. He knew that I was steaming inside, but he didn't say anything either. After breakfast, we got in the car and I drove to the meeting. It was only a ten-minute drive, but to me it felt like a lifetime. I wanted to crush and beat the hell out of myself, so my dad would feel bad.

When we arrived, I pulled up to the driveway of a huge building that I had never seen before.

After the morning of silence, my father finally said, "When we get in there, I'd like you to serve water to the people on the platform."

In anger, I lashed out saying, "Who do you think you are? Who are these people? They're Old G's (old grandpas). What do they know about my life? This meeting has nothing to do with me!"

My father got out of the car and I followed him inside

the building. When we got inside the meeting room, my father pointed to a small table with a pitcher of ice water

He said, "You go over there, take the pitcher of ice water with you and stand next to the stage"

I said, "Okay," with a ferocious attitude and did as I was told. I took a pitcher of water and stood on the platform stage with an angry face. I glanced at the door and I saw my father standing there like a statue, waiting for everyone to arrive. He inspected every person thoroughly for weapons before he let them into the room. About ten minutes later, a huge crowd filled the meeting room.

Suddenly, someone exclaimed, "Stand up! Salute our father, General Vang Pao!"

Everyone stood up and remained silent as General Vang Pao entered with all his advisors and former military personnel marching behind him. My father greeted him and guided the general to the platform. As I stood there, General Vang Pao walked up to me, looked me in the eyes, shook my hand, and said, "How are you, son?"

My hands began to shake as I mumbled, "Good!"

Although I was nervous to meet the general, my anger took over and I began to think to myself, 'Look at all of these Old G's! I'm not supposed to be here. I'm supposed to be at Disneyland having the best time of my life!'

After the general shook my hand, he walked up to the table and took his seat in the middle, with his advisors by his side.

My father came up to me and whispered in my ear, "You need to fill their cups with water and don't let them get below half."

So I rolled my eyes to the side and hissed, "Okay Dad, I'll do as you say."

I decided to play along with my dad and the Old G's. I kept filling the cups for the entire time of the meeting. As I stood still, I envisioned my friends riding the roller coaster on Space Mountain, waiting in line and having the time of their lives. And here I was listening to all the old people talking about politics.

I said to myself, "This is not fair. I can't do this anymore. I need to get out of here!"

But I did not know much back then.

I stood there with aching legs, watching for half-empty cups waiting to be filled, and listened to the discussion. Everyone wanted unification, peace and prosperous lives. I began to realize how many times these men had sacrificed their lives to protect our country and our lives. Without their compassionate hearts and many sacrifices, we would not be here in the United States of America. They had the choice to do nothing and let the Hmong perish, but because of their love and compassion for the Hmong, they endured much suffering and overcame many obstacles to set their people free. During the Vietnam War and even today, there were many people left behind enemy lines without shelter, food, and medical treatment. This literally broke my heart, "Why hadn't I thought of that?" Suddenly, it gave me a new perspective of life. Freedom was not an option in Laos and Thailand. Coming to America and living in freedom became a valuable privilege.

I had a dream to become a medical doctor, but what about the men in the room? What were their visions? I started to understand life differently.

At the end of the day, I told my dad, "Thank-you, Dad, for bringing me to the meeting. I'm sorry that I was mad and upset with you. I did not know any better. You wanted to bring me so I could learn from the elders. Thank you!"

My father just smiled.

I graduated from high school in June 1986 and received my medical assisting certificate from a class I took. My whole family attended the graduation, including my grandfather, grandmother, aunts, uncles, and cousins. It seemed like another Hmong gathering, but instead of free food and everyone suffocating in a small home, they were at my school. Everyone cheered me on as I walked the runway. I saw the joy in my parent's faces.

Toward the end of that summer, before my departure to Christ College Irvine in California, my father wanted me to meet General Vang Pao in person. My dad and I drove to General Vang Pao's home in Santa Ana, which was only 7 miles away from our house.

When I was introduced to him, he remembered me as the water boy.

He said, "Oh, you were the boy who filled our glasses with water during our last meeting, right?"

"Yes," I replied, "I was that boy."

Then he said, "You did a great job filling our glasses and you never let us go thirsty."

It was a satisfying compliment. I was so nervous sitting

across from him, however, I could feel my legs start to tremble and my speech begin to slur. He was a well-respected man with great power. My first impression of him was intimidating. I was wrong; he spoke with passion and benevolence.

Suddenly, he caught me off guard and asked me, "Son, your father brought you to see me today. Do you have any questions for me? Anything you want to ask me?"

I paused for a second; it felt like the longest second in my life.

I gulped and then asked him, "In this world, what is the one thing that will make a person's life become success-ful and prosperous?"

He paused for a moment and replied, "Son, pursue higher education and help other people. Then life will be good and prosperous," (as translated into English). I thank-ed him for his words of wisdom. On the way home I asked my father about his amazing ability to remember me. My father replied, "If you do a good deed for people, they will never forget who you are."

I engraved his words in my heart and began to under-stand my father's point of view about life. He had a plan in store for my future and knew ahead of time that this parti-cular meeting with the general would change my life for the better. This experience opened my eyes to a new world filled with compassion, love, and charitable services for other people.

CHAPTER SIX

College Life

Summer of 1986

Shortly after high school graduation, I began working as a lab technician at the University of California Irvine Medical Center. I was paid seven dollars an hour to collect specimens from the lab and deliver them to the hematology department for testing. I was given the opportunity to work with health professionals in the bone marrow biopsy lab. This life changing experience made me realize that the world of medicine was where I belonged. Many of my high school friends went their own ways to become parents, entrepreneurs, and business affiliates. For me, I was determined to go to college.

When the fall of 1986 arrived, I began my preparation for college and dorm life. My parents were against the idea of me living away at school, but I knew I had to make sacrifices to better my life. In the Hmong tradition, the youngest son must live with his parents and take care of them regardless of whether he marries or not. However, in this case, my parents were worried I wouldn't survive the real world and no one would be there to protect me. We ended up having a disagreement, leaving everyone speechless.

Eventually, my parents came to their senses and said, "You can live on your own, but you must always be careful and take good care of yourself."

I accepted their conditions.

I packed my belongings and drove to Christ College Irvine two weeks prior to class commencement for soccer camp. My overall tuition was $4,500 per semester including room and board. I was granted a scholarship for $2,000 to play for the varsity soccer team. I also received a California state grant of $2,000 per year. Even with the scholarship and grant combined, I still came short of the money needed to cover the full tuition. My parents began to make phone calls to our close relatives to get a loan to help me. In return they promised to pay them back within several months. Many relatives were reluctant to give us a loan. They gave us the impression that we would not be able to repay them because we were poor. My mom's cousins, Mr. and Mrs. Tsee Kue, had faith in me. They were kind enough to give me a $500 loan without any interest. It was a good investment in my education. Their kindness will always be treasured. My parents also went beyond their budget to pay for my books and food expenses.

Doubtful people

I began my first year of college as a pre-med student: biology major. When people asked me what I was doing in college, I replied, "I study to become a medical doctor."

Their reactions were much unexpected. They told me that studying to be a doctor was not easy, and since English was not my first language, it would be difficult for me. A close relative, who was a former teacher, told my parents that studying to be a medical doctor was impossible and that they should not waste their money investing in my pathetic dream. All the odds were against me and caused me significant emotional stress, but my parents did not lose sight of my ambition and encouraged me to follow my heart. They wanted to see me succeed and believed the path of becoming an excellent medical doctor was paved for me by God.

College Double Whammy

College was extremely challenging for me during the first couple of months. English and chemistry were not my strongest subjects. These courses required a lot of effort and time, especially English, which was not my primary language. Much of the reading and writing had to be interpreted and processed from one language to the other and back again in order for me to understand. I called it "Double English-Hmong Interpretation". I spent many hours reading textbooks, making note cards and reviewing lecture notes on a daily basis. The students and the professors were very helpful. They would take their time to sit with me and assist me when I had difficulty with homework. On top of the class work struggle, exams were even more overwhelming. When all the dorm lights were turned off, mine stayed on. I kept my goal in mind even when my body cried for sleep and my mind drifted. I knew I had to keep fighting.

At Christ College Irvine, there was a statue of Jesus with a baby lamb sitting on his feet. I named it "The Good Shepherd" because he was the one who would protect me, nurture me, and give me the guidance to fulfill my education. Each morning, I knelt down right in front of the statue and prayed to God to give me the strength to study, the knowledge to do well in classes and the wisdom to face daily obstacles. Ultimately, God was on my side. I attained the grades I sought.

Soccer Powers the Mind, the Body, and the Spirit

College gave me the opportunity to play soccer. As a freshman, I was on the varsity team filling the position of center forward. Daily I would practice from 4 pm until 6 pm with my teammates and then I would drive to Santa Ana to practice with my Hmong team for two more hours. My goal was to be the best soccer player and someday play for the Blue Thunder Team, which I had dreamed of for many years. One day while I was practicing with the "Turbo" team, the captain of the "Blue Thunder," approached me and asked me to join his team. I was shocked, but my long-held dream of playing on the "Blue Thunder" team was finally coming true.

I froze after he spoke and when I finally came to my senses I said, "Yes, I will be happy to play for the "Blue Thunder."

They appointed me the position of center forward and I scored many goals. We took first place in every tournament from southern California to northern California. There were thousands of people watching from the sidelines cheering our team on. Every time I had the ball in my possession, I could hear the crowd go wild screaming my nickname, "TURBO! TURBO! TURBO!" It was an amazing feeling! The rest was history.

Education—a Way of Life

I had to limit my friends due to the little free time I had after school, work, and soccer. I took a student work-study job at Christ College Irvine in the Admissions Department. I was paid $4.95 per hour. I performed data entry where I entered incoming student information into the school database. I also gave campus tours to prospective students and parents. The money I earned each month was barely enough for me to pay for my car, gas and insurance. I was not the wealthiest person and did not have a warm meal to eat every day, but with God's grace, I had my health and I pressed forward with everything I had.

I spent a lot of time thinking about my future and where I wanted to be in the next 10 years. I continued to envision myself as a medical doctor wearing a white coat, a stethoscope over my neck, walking down the hospital hallway and hearing my name being paged, "Dr. Xiong please come to the emergency room." I started to realize that the only way to make my dream come true was through school.

I believed *education is a collection of knowledge that makes a master key to open many doors in life.* There were many times I was physically, mentally, and spiritually drained; but the thought of how important education was empowered me with energy, motivation, and perseverance to attend classes daily and study harder. I constantly told myself there was a light at the end of every tunnel. I believed that if I set my heart to whatever I wanted, I would succeed.

Falling in Love

Two years went by quickly and the Thanksgiving weekend finally arrived. The year was 1988 and my friends invited me to attend the Thanksgiving party at my former school. I wasn't prepared to go because I had a soccer match that evening. My friends were at the Thanksgiving party and continued to call me to join them. I couldn't talk my way out of it, so I decided to drive to the party late without a date. When I arrived, everyone was dancing except for my nerdy friends. They were waiting for me at the door even though it was already 9 pm. We looked at each other and started to whisper which girl we should pick to dance with. As I glanced through the room, there was only one girl who glimmered among all the girls. I told my friends I had picked one. The band started to play soft, slow dance music. Everyone walked toward the girl they had chosen to dance with. I looked at my choice and gathered my courage as I nervously walked towards her table. She was beautiful and her eyes were glistening back at me. However, she was sitting next to her mother. Traditionally, we are not allowed to ask a girl to dance without asking her parents' permission first. Of everyone in the room, she was the only one sitting next to her mother. I was very nervous and could barely speak. I was terrified that I might be rejected and it would be the most embarrassing moment of my life, especially in front of all my friends.

I eventually swallowed my pride and asked her mother, "May I dance with your daughter?"

Her mother replied in a generous tone, "Why don't you ask her?"

I turned to the most beautiful girl and asked, "May I have this dance?"

She replied in a soft attractive tone, "Yes!"

She giggled a little as she stood up. We walked toward the dance floor and I held out my hand for her.

We began to slow dance.

She said, "My name is Choua, my last name is Yang."

I replied, "My name is Xa, my last name is Xiong."

We looked in each other's eyes and fell in love at first sight. It was electrifying!

After our first encounter, we started to date and got to know each other better. One day I took Choua and her two younger sisters to see my school. Although I did not have much money, I tried to be polite and invited them to have lunch with me in hopes that they would reject the idea. That failed miserably, when they agreed to have lunch and we stopped at a Chinese restaurant in Irvine. I ordered water for myself and a small dish for lunch. Our total lunch bill was $27.98. I only had twenty dollars in my pocket and my credit card was maxed. I started to panic and began sweating at the table. I was going to ask Choua to pitch in, but I was too embarrassed to ask. I asked Choua if I could be excused. I rushed to the bathroom. I did not have a cell phone so I used a pay phone near the bathroom to call my parents for money but unfortunately no one answered the phone. I became even more worried and felt very awkward. With my head held down I slowly walked back to our table and discovered Choua had already paid the bill.

I looked at her and said, "You didn't have to do that."

She replied, "It's all right; thank you for the wonderful time."

I was so ashamed and thanked her for what she did, saving me from embarrassment. As Choua and I got closer I began to share my dream of pursuing medicine. She wanted the same for me and was willing to give me full support.

Marrying to the Family

Mr. and Mrs. Chay Yia Yang used to live in a small, remote village near Sayaboury, Laos. They gave birth to Choua Yang in their own home and there was no birth record. They always said their children were born during the time when they planted rice or when the rice was prepared for harvest. Choua was born during Christmas time, as far as they could remember. Choua had three brothers and six sisters, with Choua the middle child. Her parents were farmers and lived a very sufficient life. One thing that she remembers ever so vividly was the poor electricity that ran through the small village. The electricity, it seemed, had a certain curfew because there was limited usage. At 8 pm it would turn on and then shut off at 11 pm, but the moon would always persuade her and her siblings to stay up late at night to play hide and seek. The moon was never alone.

Their village had no water irrigation system to bring them water. One of Choua's struggles was having to daily tread all the way to the stream and carry buckets of water on to be used for cooking and drinking. Her family always longed for rain to soothe their back breaking labor on the farm. The most memorable part of her life was coming home after a long day of farming and having a warm meal with her family. Her family always had an abundance of fruits such as mango, guava, jack fruit, durians, pineapple, bananas, and an endless menu of sweet and fresh delights until they had to emigrate to Thailand and then, to America. Leaving everything behind, she felt as if she was losing who she really was, and she was afraid to leave her home to create a new one from nothing.

Because of the early warning from General Vang Pao in 1975, Choua's father knew that they had to leave their homeland as soon as possible to avoid persecution. For a whole month, they climbed the mountains, and walked through the jungles along bumpy paths, risking their lives to emigrate to Thailand and settle in the Nam Yao Refugee Camp. The new home felt foreign and suffocating to her because of the language barriers and the new life style of captivity. Rather than the electricity curfew in Laos, there was a human curfew. If they farmed outside of the camp, they needed to return before 6 pm or else they suffered dire consequences. Those unfortunate stories should never leave the camp. She can still recall being only seven, seeing the dust fill the air as everyone rushed to the gates as the ear-piercing siren rang through the air marking the end of the day.

She lived in Thailand for four years, feeling as though she would never be able to settle down. Then she discovered that she and her family could emigrate to America. They arrived in Orange County, California in 1979.

Living in Thailand had been a huge change, but living in America, where a majority of the population was Caucasian and the language was English, felt like living in an alternate universe. When she first attended Van Buren Elementary School, in 5th grade, she was very nervous. All of the American students congregated among themselves, isolating from other students. She was often bullied by them. A very clear image etched in her memory of a girl in her class pouring grains from the sandbox on her head. Choua's confident state of mind crumbled that day, but as she wept her way back home, her father said some truly encouraging words, "If they slap one side of your face, you should turn the other side and let them slap that side too."

At that age, it was hard for her to understand, because she felt it wasn't right to let people step all over you. But as time progressed, she thought hard and realized that her father was a peacemaker. He didn't believe in battling with life, because fighting fire with fire, only causes more problems. Her father believed she shouldn't waste her energy by fighting back, because, in the end, that would make her just as horrible as the sand box girl.

Choua wanted to succeed in life; always worked hard, and cared diligently for her family. During the time that she attended Valencia High School in Placentia, California, she struggled with what she wanted for her future. She studied and carefully saved her money from cleaning homes, baby-sitting, and working desk jobs. She dreamed of becoming a nurse one day, but as she conversed with her counselor, he unfortunately shattered her dream. She was told that she was not strong enough to lift 200-300 pound patients because of her small frame and height. As she heard those words, everything around her shattered and her dream of becoming a nurse vanished in the blink of an eye. So she searched for a different path.

While attending high school with uncertainty about her future, she tagged along with one of her friends, who was seeking a fortune teller about her future life. Her friend questioned the fortune teller about her future and wondered what type of man she would marry. The fortune teller replied that her husband would be a doctor and her life would be happy ever after. Choua sat quietly and listened to the fortune teller's word of wisdom. In Choua's mind, she wanted that to be her fortune. She would not mind marrying a handsome doctor, but she knew that in order to obtain a good life she must always work hard and be a good person.

She attended the National Education Private School and graduated with an associate's degree in accounting.

Destiny changed her life. She was a very strong; independent woman and her confidence made me love her even more. She always went out of her way, above and beyond, to pursue anything that came across her path.

Building a Marriage

We took our marriage vows while I was a junior in college. In the Hmong tradition, the groom was the main financial source for the wedding cost. Life was a challenge and finances scarce, but love conquered all. I borrowed money from my parents, grand-parents, and aunt to fund our wedding, with a promise to pay them back. We had a traditional Hmong wedding at Choua's parents' home in Placentia. We did not have a wedding party at that time, or go on a honeymoon, because we only had enough money to cover the wedding cost. Every day, I was so thankful to have met Choua and to be her husband. Without her encouraging words and praise, I would have been lost. We both worked very diligently over the following summer and throughout the year. Finally, we were able to save enough money to fully fund our wedding party after our first child, Elizabeth—named after Queen Elizabeth II—was born. Choua suffered as much as I did. She worked diligently eight to nine hours a day, and took care of our daughter while I managed to attend school with a part-time work-study job. We were very thankful to have my parents and my aunt to care for our daughter while we were out working and studying. Choua worked a full time job to put food on the table and to pay the bills. She made eight dollars an hour and strove daily, working, working, and working. Though she would come home totally exhausted, she sacrificed much, demonstrating her affection love for me and our daughter.

We did not have any medical insurance to cover our family; so knowing that anyone could get sick at any time was very frightening. Happily, there was a wonderful doctor in our lives, Dr. Lutsky, who cared deeply for the poor and helped many people without charging a huge medical bill. It only cost us fifteen dollars per visit. God was always watching over our family and thankfully no one encountered any serious medical illnesses that required hospitalization. My wife, Choua, and daughter, Elizabeth, meant the world to me. They were the cheerleaders and supporters in my career. Choua gave the ultimate sacrifice for me. Every day when I woke up and saw Choua lying next to me and our daughter, I felt at peace, knowing that we would always there for each other. I found her so young at heart and always driven with life, especially when it came to caring for us. Although she was unable to fulfill her dream of becoming a nurse, she always believed that our daughter and future children would become doctors. They would be her courage, strength, and love. She was hard-working and spent her time doing the smallest deeds that others may have disregarded. I was very fortunate to have Choua as my wife, mother of my child, life partner in adventure, and my best friend.

CHAPTER SEVEN

Dual Degree: Chiropractic and Medicine

Applying to Chiropractic School

When my senior year at Christ College Irvine came to an end, I started to search for medical schools. There were four major admissions criteria required before the interview process: an outstanding cumulative grade point average (GPA), a high Medical College Admission Test (MCAT) score (25 or higher), an exceptional letter of recommendation, and community or hospital volunteer work hours. My GPA was sufficient. I had excellent volunteer hours and experience, and exceptional letters of recommendation from my undergraduate professors. Before applying to medical school, I would have to take the MCAT with a score of 25 or higher. I did not know how to prepare for the exam and did not understand the registration process. The road ahead was foggy with no obvious signs of guidance or support. Unfortunately, I had missed the deadline to apply for medical school and felt miserable. Choua comforted me and told me, "God is preparing you for many great things; you must be patient." I knelt down in front of "The Good Shepherd" statue at Christ College Irvine and prayed, asking for a new direction. One week later, there was a career day at our college. I walked along the cracked sidewalk, passing by numerous tables arrayed in vibrant colors and decorated with huge foldable posters, pens, papers, and on some there was even candy. There were so many career opportunities, it was overwhelming. As I sighed and began to walk away, and a big white sign caught my attention. The sign read "Los Angeles College of Chiropractic." On the bottom it said, "Doctor of Chiropractic."

"What is a doctor of chiropractic?" I quietly mumbled to myself.

As I approached the booth, there was a gentleman standing behind the table who asked me, "Would you some information about becoming a doctor of chiropractic?"

I tilted my head and raised an eyebrow "Sure!" I said. He further exclaimed that he was a doctor of chiropractic, so I sked him, "What is a doctor of chiropractic?"

The doctor replied, "A doctor of chiropractic is often referred to as a chiropractor or a chiropractic physician, one who practices with a hands-on approach to health care that includes: patient examination, diagnosis, and chiropractic treatment, including physical therapy and rehabilitative exercises, as well as nutritional, dietary and lifestyle counseling."

I wasn't sure what he meant, so I requested more information about the program.

"Can you tell me more?" I asked.

"Yes," he responded. "You perform a physical examination, make a diagnosis, and treat the patient with chiropractic manipulation."

He went on to explain how he used his hands to palpate the spine and apply "chiropractic adjustment" to restore joint mobility, thereby alleviating pain and muscle tightness, while allowing the tissue to heal. At the end of our conversation, he gave me a brochure about the Los Angeles College of Chiropractic (LACC) program. I was very much intrigued by the information.

I reread the information numerous times when I got to the dorm. The more I read, the more I became interested in pursuing a career in chiropractic medicine. I discussed the idea with Choua and she was very supportive. We knew this must be a calling from the Lord. He was paving an alternative opportunity for me to become a doctor. We both agreed and spoke to my parents. They stood in silence as I expressed my thoughts and without hesitation they said, "Son, if this is something you see yourself doing for the rest of your life, you should pursue it." With both my parents and Choua by my side, I began the application process for the LACC admissions department. Approximately a month later, I received a letter for an interview.

My life was about to change as my father and I drove to the LACC Campus for my interview. When we arrived at the campus, I was not impressed at all. It was not an ordinary university campus with all the tall buildings as I had anticipated. I found myself wondering if I really wanted to be there for the next three years of my life. My father advised me that I should not judge a book without reading it, and told me to proceed with my interview. I took a chance and did it.

There were three doctors who interviewed me. They asked me why I wanted to pursue a career as a doctor of chiropractic. They also asked if I planned to make a lot of money. The very last question was, "If we grant your admission to our program, would you like to pursue it?" I answered the questions appropriately and afterwards, we took a tour of the campus. I was given the opportunity to talk to several students on the tour, and their responses were very positive.

A month later, I received a letter stating "Congratulations! You have been accepted to the Doctor of Chiropractic Accelerated Program at Los Angeles College of Chiropractic for the Class of 1994 and we look forward to seeing you in the fall."

Graduating from College

May of 1991 came and I finished my senior year of undergrad school. I walked the stage to receive my bachelor's degree in biology with a minor in chemistry. My whole family attended the graduation ceremony. There were more than thirty people cheering me on as I received my degree. My parents were so proud of me that day.

My father approached me after the ceremony and said, "Son, you are the first one in our family to receive a bachelor's degree. Your success is our success."

I could see the happy tears in his eyes; it was a joyous moment for both of us and the whole family. My father desired to host a big celebration party for me, but due to financial burdens, he was not able to do so.

Choua and I worked diligently over the summer to save money for a post-graduation celebration party; however, due to the financial constraints in our lives, we were not able to do so. The summer of hard work went by quickly and it was time for the next chapter in my life to unfold.

Attending Los Angeles College of Chiropractic

The day after Labor Day 1991, my chiropractic career began. On the first day of class, there were over one hundred students enrolled in the doctor of chiropractic accelerated program. In our gross anatomy class, we were separated into groups of ten and each group was assigned to a cadaver. Our first encounter with the cadaver was a day to remember. Many students were either very nervous or were appalled by the odor. My exposure to the Vietnam War and losing my older brother and little sister prepared me for the harsh reality of death. My group anxiously walked into the freezer prepared to choose one of the ten cadavers covered in a clear plastic bag. We chose a male and brought him over to our station. We first prayed and asked the cadaver to teach us, forgive us, and to give us the blessing of knowledge and wisdom to help cure the living. We named him "Frank." He was an elderly Caucasian male with a full head of white hair. He was probably in his early 80's but his frame was well built for his age. I began to imagine his life before his passing. Maybe he was a jubilant grandfather with grandchildren or possibly a lonely old man who could not pay for his own burial.

The smell of formaldehyde filled the gross anatomy lab. Students were pinching their noses and wearing masks. They described the order as rotten eggs. I, on the other hand, was not bothered so much. I was thrilled to have the opportunity to study the human body so I could help the living.

We started to dissect Frank from the head, neck, chest, abdomen, and extremities. Calmly, I helped carry out the dissection with a firm composure. First, we identified every single nerve, blood vessel, bone, muscle, and organ. There was much to learn from the human body in preparation for our interim exams, given in both oral and Scantron format. All of the classes were difficult, but gross anatomy was the most intense and by far the most complex subject. I stayed with Frank late at night, constantly reviewing for each of the exams. There were nights when I would wake up at two o'clock in the morning to read for a couple of hours and then go back to sleep, only to wake up a few hours later to study some more.

Every day, I drove an hour just to get to school. When traffic backed up, I would take out my flashcards and review my notes. On several occasions, I experienced near death encounters with car accidents. Providentially for me, I made it back home all in one piece. My classmates and I would stay up late with Frank in the cadaver lab. If we had spare time, we would grab a bite to eat and then continue our studies until three o'clock in the morning before our exam. One night one of my classmates came over to my house to study for an oral anatomy exam. He and I quietly reviewed our notes and before we knew it, the sun rose. Out of panic, we raced to school, however, due to the lack of sleep we felt like zombies. Our eyes were deeply sunken in and our faces were as pale as Frank's. Our first exam was at eight o'clock in the morning. My classmate and I were completely absent-minded and utterly exhausted.

One of the professors pointed to the cadaver and asked us, "What is the largest organ in the human body?"

We were puzzled as we looked at each other with confusion and blurted, "The liver?"

We both answered incorrectly. The correct answer was obviously the skin. When the exam ended, we left the room in embarrassment. All the hard work and studying did not pay off. We quickly learned from our mistake and prepared more effectively for future exams.

During my second year, our first son, Einstein—named after physicist Albert Einstein—was born. It was very difficult to take care of two children while being a full-time student. My wife was only making eight dollars an hour and had to work numerous hours of overtime to cover our expenses and bills. I took out many school loans to pay for my tuition and to cover some of our expenses. Many times, Choua and I were both exhausted from the workload. I even thought about quitting school and getting a regular job to help my family, but Choua was always positive about my schooling and demanded that I continue my education. She constantly reminded me that the struggle today would only bring us one day closer the success of a lifetime. She was always energetic and worked very hard to support the family.

I studied hard, and managed to receive A's and B's in my first two years of chiropractic school. My third year came quickly and I began my internship at the Whittier Health Clinic. I was seeing patients on a daily basis. This was a very exciting challenge because every day brought new people with unique and interesting medical cases into my life. I truly enjoyed my internship rotation as a chiropractic intern.

During my exit interview, my chiropractic clinician, Dr. Ahmed, said, "I don't see you practicing as a chiropractor, but I do see you driving a Mercedes Benz."

Receiving Doctor of Chiropractic Degree

Prior to my graduation, I had to take the National Board of Chiropractic Examiners (NBCE) Examination. I spent many hours away from Choua and our children to study for my exam. If I were lucky, I would see our children right before they went to bed. The stress and worry brought me many doubts. Choua and I would pray every night, asking God for strength and guidance.

Many times when I opened my books to study, I would say, "What if I don't pass my board exams? I won't be able to practice. I will have wasted all of my time, effort, and money for nothing. Most importantly, I won't be able to fulfill my dream to the fullest extent."

Choua and I knew that God was always listening to our

prayers. He was the hope that kept all of us going, especially during the most uncertain times of our lives. With much hard work, dedication, perseverance, and God's helping hand, I was able to pull through and passed the NBCE Examinations on the very first try.

Towards the end of my third year in chiropractic school, I came across another major obstacle, the California Board of Chiropractic Examiners Examination for licensing. Choua and I were still poor and financially unstable. Our second beautiful daughter was then born. She was our little pumpkin and we named her Emily—after a famous American poet, Emily Dickinson. Although all of our children smiled and filled our home with their joyous laughs, we felt fear piling up upon our shoulders. All we could ever ask for was their good health and happiness. We wanted to show our children a brighter world and I always wanted to be a positive role model for them.

Inconveniently, I had to take my exam in San Jose, California. It was going to be a strenuous seven-hour drive and my examination was going to take nearly a day to complete. Choua and I were concerned financially and we prayed to God, asking for a light to show us the way through the dark tunnel. Our prayer was answered with an unexpected call from one of my classmates. He asked me if I wanted to join the rest of the classmates and rent a hotel room in San Jose to prepare for the board exam.

I immediately exclaimed, "Sign me in!"

There were fifteen of us and we rented a small studio apartment for three nights. Each person only had to pay ten dollars per day. The most comical remembrance from this experience was one of my classmates brought his small electric rice cooker to feed us every day. Although it was just one room, the company of many others with similar aspirations made the atmosphere livelier.

Everyone managed to pass the exam, except for one of my classmates and myself. Overall, I did very well but failed two points short on the chiropractic adjustment procedure portion. I felt miserable. I felt like a disappointment to my family.

It was this moment when I started to doubt myself, questioning myself, "I studied extremely hard, so why is this is happening to me? Why me? Why me?" If I only knew what plans God had in store for me behind those closed doors, I would not have been so fixated on picking myself apart. Though I suffered tremendously from this experience, I learned equally from it as well. I revitalized myself, studied for the next three long months, retook the board exam and passed without difficulty!

December 1994, my graduation day finally arrived. The dream I had longed for was finally here. My entire family was at the graduation with glistening eyes of bliss. I wore my doctoral cap and gown, and marched on the stage to receive my doctorate of chiropractic degree. The excitement rushed through my body like lightning. Luckily, I didn't go into shock as I stood on stage in front of my family, friends, and professors. The administrators, faculty, and clinicians swore me in—"From now on you shall be called Doctor of Chiropractic." This was one of the most gratifying moments of my life. My wife and parents hosted a graduation party to celebrate my accomplishment at a local Chinese restaurant in Santa Ana, California.

I joined another chiropractic physician in Santa Ana where we provided a full scope of chiropractic care and physical therapy. Primarily, I was enjoying my time providing chiropractic care to my patients, but I felt emptiness in the pit of stomach even though I wasn't hungry. I knew I was still incapable of providing a full range of medical practice to my patients. My dream of becoming a medical doctor and walking through the hallways of a hospital continued to replay in my mind everyday like a broken record. I would close my eyes and picture my pager going off again, alerting me to report to the nurses' station, the obstetric ward, the intensive care unit, the operating room and the emergency room. I even visualized myself being paged over the intercom. The voice would say, "Dr. Xiong, please come to the ER. Dr. Xiong, please come to the ER." These visions began to haunt me. I was reminded of my brother and the life we had before coming to America. The thought clung to my heart and I knew I was cheating myself, settling for less than what I was capable of.

Returning of the Dream

My wife and I were actually making a living, but I began questioning my dream. I wanted to offer more to my family financially as well as to follow my dream of becoming a successful medical doctor. I spoke to Choua and she fully supported the idea of letting me go back to school—medical school. She reminded me that since we made it through once, we could make it through again. With Choua aboard, I started to look into medical schools. Medical school in the United States would be a problem since we didn't have any savings; it would cost more than a few of my organs to attend. I heard that one of my chiropractic colleagues was accepted to one of the medical schools in the Caribbean. I spoke to him and was encouraged to apply to that school, Ross University School of Medicine, located in the Dominican Republic. I submitted my application and two months later I received a letter for an interview. I confidently went through the interview process and it seemed like a very positive one in the end. One month later, I received my letter of acceptance. Choua and I sent a thousand dollars to secure my place at the University.

I was thrilled and said, "Finally, I will become what I've always dreamed of, a medical doctor!"

However, I did not realize how far I had to travel and what it would feel like to live three thousand miles away from my family. I became anxious and eventually fell into depression.

The summer of 1996 came to an aching end. It was time for me to get on the plane and fly to the Dominican Republic for my medical education, and I was not prepared. My family needed me and I was running out of time.

Choua looked me in the eyes and said, "You are going to medical school to become a medical doctor; you are not going to war, so don't worry about it. You will come back alive."

I had never been separated from my family before, especially from my wife and my children, for such a great amount of time and distance. I was still heavily conflicted. I had no choice, however, since we had already secured my seat with the thousand dollars.

Choua said, "You must go. I know deep down in my heart you will succeed. You don't have to worry about our kids and me. I will protect them with my life."

She had so much confidence in me. She believed in me one hundred percent and also found the funds to buy me a plane ticket. I was so blessed to have married such a strong woman. She supported me with the strength of a whole army of encouraging soldiers.

Medical School and Home Again

When my departure date arrived, it was very hard to say goodbye to Choua, my three children, and my parents. They all came to the Los Angeles International Airport to send me off. I stared at Choua and our three kids— Elizabeth, Einstein, and Emily; the heaviness in my heart and the lump in my throat grew, choking back my tears.

An awful thought suddenly appeared in my mind: "Choua will be without a husband and my three kids will be without a father. What kind of life will they live without me?"

I prayed that God would watch over them and keep each one safe until I returned. It was time to board the plane. I hugged everyone and started walking through the corridor with tears rushing through my eyes. The uneasiness stirred in my body when I turned around and took one last glimpse at my family. I wondered how each of them was feeling about me leaving. As my plane quickened and lifted off the runway, I couldn't stop thinking about Choua and our kids. I asked myself about the importance of marriage and family in comparison to my dream of becoming a medical doctor. It was clear to me that I couldn't leave my family no matter how much I wanted too. My anxiety level was off the charts. The pounding in my heart began to race and I couldn't breathe. I was suffocating and panicky. Suddenly my nose started to bleed. The flight attendant spotted me shakily wiping my nose with my hands so she gave me a facial towel and a bottle of water to calm my nerves. The four-hour flight to Miami for the connecting flight seemed like forever. As soon as we landed at the Miami International Airport, I picked up the pay phone and called Choua.

I said to her, "I'm coming home! I'm not going to medical school."

I sensed her slight relief as she said, "Honey, come home."

Immediately, I started looking for flights back to Los Angeles, but there were no flights available. The flight clerk said that I could take a flight to Puerto Rico and then to Los Angeles. I got on the first flight to Puerto Rico and took the next connecting flight back to Los Angeles. I felt miserably regretful, but I couldn't wait to see my family again. Choua, our kids, and my parents were waiting for me as I came out of the flight corridor. I embraced them and said I would never leave them ever again. Tears streamed down our faces and everyone was happy that I returned. Although I felt relieved about being back with my family, I was very disappointed in myself. I had wasted so much time and money just to return home.

A few days later, I found a job in data entry to make enough money to pay the bills. My confidence was very low and I felt discouraged. I kept telling myself that my dream was not to work like a normal person, but to provide medical care to people as a doctor. My ambition was still to pursue a medical education and become a medical doctor no matter what.

I worked hard but made little money to support my family. Choua and I never really had much money since we got married but God always watched over our family, providing enough finances and blessings to keep us moving with our lives. There were times when we didn't have any money at all and suddenly people would send us a check or we would get a refund in the mail. We made it through, one day at a time. By January of 1997, I began to envision my dreams of becoming a medical doctor again. I knew we were poor because of my debt and I felt like a failure. I began to search for medical schools in the Caribbean again. I came across Spartan Health Sciences University, School of Medicine, in Veux Fort, Saint Lucia. The tuition was reasonable and affordable. I shared the idea of going back to medical school with Choua and she was fully supportive.

She said, "This time, make the right decision, go for it and you shall succeed."

I took her words and filled out the admission application. About six weeks later, I received a phone call to set up a phone interview. The interview with the dean went pretty well, given my background as a doctor of chiropractic and the dream of pursuing a medical doctorate. I was told over the phone that I had been accepted to their doctor of medicine (MD) program. He welcomed me to the graduating class of 2000. I started to prepare for departure but continued to have terrifying flash backs about leaving my family again. Choua noticed my anxiety and depression so she took a different approach to help me overcome my negative thoughts.

She repeated, "You are going to medical school to become a medical doctor; you are not going to war, so don't worry about it. You will come back alive. This time you will succeed."

It was Labor Day of 1997. I was more prepared to handle my emotions, anxiety, and depression. I promised Choua and our kids that I would call them every night. I also told them that although my body would not be physically with them; my spirit would always be their guide. I boarded the American Airlines plane at the Los Angeles International Airport and flew to Miami, from Miami to Puerto Rico, and finally from Puerto Rico to the island of Saint Lucia.

Attending Medical School in the Caribbean

We landed at Hewanorra International Airport in Saint Lucia late in the evening; I developed severe anxiety and became homesick. By the time I picked up my luggage and checked in at the airport hotel it was already 11 pm. I called Choua to let her know that I arrived but it took an unexpected turn as soon as I heard her voice.

I quickly said, "I am coming back home tomorrow!"

Choua said, "You're not coming home! This is the second time! You will do fine. I have full confidence in you."

She calmed me down and comforted my fears. I knelt down and prayed that God would give me the strength to overcome the negative thoughts in my head and my heart. I couldn't sleep through the night. I was constantly tossing, turning, and thinking about my family. I thought that night would never end.

Fortunately, the sun rose and I had to check out from the hotel. I dragged my two large suitcases with me to the hotel lobby and asked for a taxi cab. As I waited for the cab to arrive, I started to feel anxious with steaming frustration. One hour later the taxi finally came. Thankfully, the cab driver was very nice and dropped me off at Spartan Health Sciences University School of Medicine in the least amount of time. The medical school building was not what I had expected. It was an old building with four classrooms including a gross anatomy lab. There was no air conditioning. The anatomy lab was filled with hot, humid air and formaldehyde fumes. After that scene, I was again determined to go to the airport and take the first flight back to the United States. As I looked at the other students, I could sense that they were all thinking the same thing.

I discovered that one of my classmates had three children and a wife just like me. He also left his family to fulfill his dream of becoming a medical doctor. We chatted for some time and got acquainted with one another. He had already found a small house and was looking for a roommate. I told him that I was looking for a place to live. He kindly offered, "If you want to, you can stay in the spare room." He added that it would cost one hundred dollars per month. I responded that I would take it because I desperately needed a place to live. He was from the U.S. Virgin Islands and had lived in Florida for quite some time before he decided to attend medical school.

I dragged my two big suitcases all the way to his rental house. The bedroom was super small, barely fitting a full size mattress. There was a small cabinet with a mirror on the top. I told myself it was better than sleeping at the hotel and being alone. I started to feel at ease and safe for once.

The first day at medical school was not impressive. We did not receive a cadaver because our cadaver was still being ordered. In addition, medical school was not what I had expected. There were twenty-nine of us that enrolled as MS1 (medical student year one). We all had left our families in United States, and we were all stressed out from the living situation. Medical school was not easy. Some students did very well while other students failed. With my background as a doctor of chiropractic, I was able to sail through the first semester. The four months went by quickly and I took my final exams. Before I knew it, I was at the airport waiting to go home.

The first trip back home after four months on the island was a treasure. As I walked out of the plane at the Los Angeles International Airport, I saw my family: Choua, Einstein, Elizabeth, Emily, and my parents. I was excited to see everyone. My break was only a week long, but we went to the movies, stayed up late at night to talk, and caught up with my children's school work. Time, however, flew by. In the blink of an eye, it was time to go back to Saint Lucia. We went through the same emotional rollercoaster but this time it was slightly easier than before. Nothing, however, hurt more than leaving my family behind.

Second semester of school was rough. I spent many hours reading textbooks and taking many exams. Days passed, months went by, and then finally, after one long year, it was time to go home for good. I was so thrilled that I packed all my belongings in my suitcases before my final exams even began. I took my last final and then proceeded with the medical exit exam before leaving. I scored high on all the exams and was certified by the dean of academics for completing my first two years of medical school.

Leaving Saint Lucia for Good

During the sixteen months in which I lived in Saint

Lucia, I had developed many friendships with the local people. A nice family who always welcomed me into their home for food and company basically adopted me. The evening before my departure back to California, they hosted a feast and congratulated me for finishing the first two years of medical school. I thanked each and every one for their hospitality and for protecting me from harm during my stay at Saint Lucia. Without them, life would have been very difficult and perhaps, I would not have completed my medical education. Forever I will treasure those moments that I spent with them on the island. It was hard to say goodbye to everyone, but I had to return to my family in California. The night before my flight was filled with happiness and anxiety. I had a hard time sleeping, of course. At 5:30 am I rushed out of bed and awakened my roommate. For some reason, he had to remain behind on the island for the next two weeks to write his exams before he could go home to his family in Florida. It was very sad that I had to leave him behind. He was like a brother to me; I saw a lot of myself in him. We created a brotherly bond and enjoyed each other's company especially with our families being so far away.

As I got into the taxi, I glanced back and saw him waving goodbye. It tore my heart apart and tears ran down my face. I kept looking back at him, our small house, and our neighbor's kids. They were my family now.

My plane did not leave until one in the afternoon, and yet, by seven in the morning, I was already at the airport among my other classmates.

We talked, we laughed, and we exclaimed with excitement, "Finally we are going home!"

Everyone was enthusiastic and we could hardly wait to board the plane. At the same time, we were sad that we had to depart from one another. Perhaps we would never see each other ever again. It was very hard to say goodbye. Finally, we were called to board the American Airlines plane. As it took off, we all looked out the window to view the city of Vaux Forte for the very last time. I sadly said, "Goodbye Saint Lucia."

Our plane landed in Miami, and unfortunately my connecting flight had a layover until the morning. I did not have money to pay for a hotel room, so I slept on the airport chair for six hours in the chilly terminal. I took the very first flight out of Miami at 6 am to Los Angeles. I was tired and exhausted, but happy that I was on my way home for good. After a long flight, my plane finally landed at LAX. As I stepped off the plane and marched through the corridor, I saw my three children, Choua, and both my mom and dad eagerly waiting for my arrival. As soon as I came out of the passageway, all my kids ran to me, hugged me, and welcomed me back home. Tears streamed down my face. As we were driving home, I stared at the blue sky through the window and thanked God for bringing me home safely.

Captain Yong Ge Xiong—My Father

Yer Kue-Hang—My Mother

Chay Yia Yang—My Father-in-law

Say Thao—My Mother-in-law

My father, Captain Yong Ge Xiong - 2nd from the right
Long Cheng, Laos, 1970.

Left to right, Law Lue, Law Toua, and Law Xang Xiong
Long Cheng, Laos 1970.

Our buses leaving Ban Vinai Refugee Camp, 1980.
Photo: Captain Yong Ge Xiong's Collection

PAN AM journeyed to the United States of America, 1980.
Artist: Tisha Hang

Xa received his Medical Assisting Certificate Grandpa, Xa, Dad
Santa Ana, California, 1986.

Soccer powered the Mind, the Body and the Spirit.
Captain of the Varsity Soccer Team, Christ College Irvine, CA 1988.

"Nerd", college sophomore, 1988.

GENERAL CATALOG 1988-89

Christ College
Irvine Catalog, 1988.

Xa & Choua
Hmong New Year, Santa Ana 1988.

Xa received his BA degree
Concordia University Irvine

Xa received his Doctor of
Chiropractic (DC)
Los Angeles College of
Chiropractic, Whittier, CA 1994

Xa attended Spartan Health Sciences University
School of Medicine, St. Lucia, 1997.

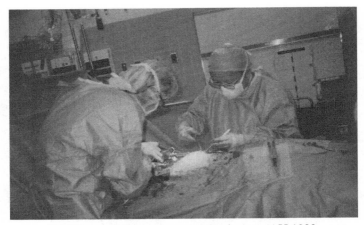

Dr. Xiong performed surgery, Anchorage, AK 1999.

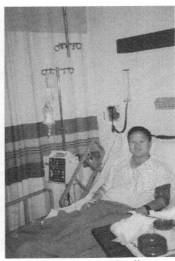

Dr. Xiong's 1st delivery, a boy!   Stomach ulcer bleeding
West Houston Medical Center
Houston, TX 2000.

Dr. Xa Xiong Family, Santa Ana, California - 2001.
Back row left to right: Elizabeth, Xa, Choua, Einstein
Middle row left to right: Aunt Shoua, Capt. Yong Ge Xiong,
Yer Kue-Hang, Emily
Front row left to right: Elena, Alexander

Captain Yong Ge Xiong
Dr. Xa Xiong, DC, MD

"Father and Son"

The Post-Crescent, July 19, 2005
University of Wisconsin
Fox Valley Family Medicine Residency Program
Appleton, Wisconsin

Dr. Xiong received a
"High Educational Achievement Award"
from the Xiong United Inc., MN 2009.

Dr. Xiong received the "JOURNEY OF HOPE AWARD—for outstanding achievement by a refugee during resettlement and integration into American society" by Secretary Eloise Anderson, at the State Capitol, Madison, Wisconsin, June 18th, 2011.

Dr. Xiong spoke to the audiences.
Wisconsin, 2014

I thank God for the countless blessings in my
life and the opportunity to wake up every morning and
save lives. Through God, anything is possible. I became the
American Dream.

"Life is like a lock of treasures; your task is to find the KEY, so
you can unlock and fulfill your dreams."

"Education [ej-oo-**KEY**-shuh n] is a collection of knowledge
that makes up a master **KEY** to open many doors in life."

"Through education, the seemingly impossible dream becomes
possible."

"Im~possible"

This book is dedicated to my beloved Father—
Captain Yong Ge Xiong
"The greatest gift is LOVE"
AND
my Mother—Yer Kue-Hang
"Education is created by humans and not by evil...it is learnable."

<u>CHAPTER EIGHT</u>

Critical Moments

Clinical Rotation—El Paso, Texas

I was relieved and excited to be home. However, the journey of medical school was not over yet. I was home for about a month and was able to spend a lot of time with my family. Even so, it was still stressful to think that I would have to go back to complete my third and fourth year medical rotations. The day arrived in the blink of the eye, I filled my suitcases again, but I would not be leaving the country. This time I was headed to El Paso, Texas. The anxious feeling of being separated from my family began to kick in again. I placed my suitcases into my car and said good-bye to my wife, kids, and parents. I could see the tears in Choua's eyes and our children's eyes when I gave them hugs and kisses before I drove off.

I got on US Highway 10 before sunrise and headed east toward El Paso, Texas. It was a sad and lonely long drive. I arrived in El Paso late in the evening. I stayed in an inexpensive motel near Highway 10 until the next day. It was scary, but much better than sleeping in the car alone. I did not want Choua and our kids to worry so I called to let them know that I had arrived safely and was staying in a very nice hotel. I didn't sleep throughout the night and worried about Choua and our kids. The next day I went apartment hunting. I was able to find a small studio apartment on the second floor located on Mesa Drive. The apartment was not furnished and I had no mattress, table, or a chair to sit on. I had less than fifty dollars in my wallet. Luckily, Choua packed a bed sheet that I could lay on the carpet so I could sleep. She also gave me one blank check for my apartment deposit not to exceed three hundred dollars. I had fifty dollars in my wallet to survive the month. I went down to the apartment dumpster and discovered that someone had just moved out and left behind an old desk and a broken roller chair. They were old but still durable. To others, these were trash but to me they were treasures. I fixed the roller chair with several screws and wiped the desk clean. I thanked God for everything he had provided for me; a roller chair and a desk so that I could sit and study. I did not have a mattress, so I slept on the carpet throughout my rotations. Life was difficult, but livable.

Hospital Training—Juarez de Mexico

Our training hospital site was located in Juarez de Mexico. I had to drive over the international bridge to get to Juarez. Prior to entering Mexico, I had to have an American passport and an entry permit. I went to the immigration consulate in El Paso and applied for an entry permit. The immigration process went very slow, so I waited for one week before I received the permit. The first time traveling to Mexico by myself was nerve racking, but yet a bit second nature to me since I had lived in St. Lucia. At the time, Juarez was listed as one of the most dangerous cities in the world due to the drug cartel war. There were police officers everywhere inspecting every single car as I crossed the border between the United States and Mexico. I found myself hoping that nothing would happen. Happily, I made it across safely!

When I arrived in the city, I could not find the hospital. I did not have a global positioning system (GPS). I asked several local people to help me, but no one could give me directions. I didn't speak Spanish and the street people did not know English. The people in Juarez were very different and so was their culture. I was hoping that the locals would be friendly, but I was an unknown entity. I was afraid and felt lost for a while. I ended up buying a map and managed to find the hospital after two hours of searching. I found my way to the front door of the hospital where there was a security guard standing at the door. I asked him if I could speak to someone in charge of the medical student rotation. He replied in Spanish, so I did not understand. I just began walking down to the receptionist's desk. Thankfully, I found several of my colleagues talking to the receptionist and I joined them. We were promptly guided to the medical student office by the receptionist. We were given orientation to the hospital and completed our paperwork for our rotations.

My first rotation was cardiology (study of the heart). I

was guided by one of the Spanish nurses to my preceptor's office. When we arrived, the doctor's door was closed. I stood outside and waited for two hours. Eventually one of the nurses came by and said, "The doctor will not be coming in today," and told me to go home and come back the next day. It was such a waste of time, but that was how things were done in Mexico; time was not an issue for them. Doctors came and went at any time. I drove back to El Paso with much frustration and disappointment. As I approached the checkpoint at the U.S. and Mexican border, there was a truck about two cars ahead of me that was stopped by the Mexican officers. There were dogs and many officers rushing to the truck. Guns were pointed and voices were yelling at the truck. More than ten people with children came out when the officer opened the door. The incident gave me a flashback to the time when my family and I were in Laos at the Hin Heup Bridge—the communists were shooting innocent people. All the traffic was detained. The weather was hot and humid and sweat dripped down on my face as we all waited. Providentially, after an hour, the checkpoints were reopened. I thanked God for everyone's safety. I finally crossed the border without harm and returned safely to my apartment.

The next day I woke up at six o'clock with fear of going back to Juarez. I told myself not to drive back to Mexico. I sat in my apartment and had many thoughts about the long treacherous road of studying day and night, as well as my family's sacrifices. I was alone with much anxiety. I prayed and asked God to give me direction and guidance.

All of a sudden I felt a strange sensation in my gut telling me to go back to Juarez, Mexico for my rotation. I could sense the peace in my heart that God was watching over me and there would be no harm upon my travel to Juarez.

I picked up my backpack and drove to Juarez. Crossing over to Mexico was frightening but I arrived without any problem. Once I got to the hospital, my attending cardiologist was already in his office. He handed me an agenda and told me his schedule. He had a few procedures, including a pacemaker placement that was performed in an unsterilized fashion. The patient survived the procedure. We made a few rounds in the ICU, as well as the in-patient unit. My first day was finally over! It was three o'clock in the afternoon. The cardiologist told me he had to go play golf, so I should go back to El Paso before the traffic jammed.

I drove back and forth to Juarez, Mexico for three long months. In addition, living alone in El Paso gave me the opportunity to study for the United States Medical Licensing Examination (USMLE). In order to meet the requirements to take the USMLE Step 1, a medical student must complete the first two years from an accredited medical school and have the approval of the dean in order to register. I fulfilled all of the requirements. As a foreign medical student, I would have to file my application through the Educational Commission for Foreign Medical Graduates (ECFMG) to take the exam. The entire process took about three months. During that time, I spent many hours reviewing medical text books, notes, and the *First Aid for The USMLE Step 1* by Tao Le and Vikas Bhushan. Regrettably, I was not aware that there were practice questions in preparation for the board. No one gave me any tips how to advance to prepare myself for the USMLE. I had to learn the hard way and forced myself to study everything there was to know. Three months passed by and it was time to take the examination in downtown El Paso. I was very worried and couldn't sleep the night before. At most, I only had two hours of good sleep. I awoke at 6:30 am, showered, ate a piece of white toast, and drove to the test site. I got lost on the way and became very distressed. Finally, I managed to arrive at the test site ten minutes before the start time. Most of my classmates were already checked in. Everyone looked nervous and apprehensive with fear of failing the exam. We encouraged each other to take the exam using all the medical knowledge we had learned from medical school and clinical rotations.

As we were about to take the exam one of the proctors announced that, "This will be the last paper exam given. After today all future exams will be computerized."

With this, we were all nervous and became even more distressed. The entire exam took eight long hours with one hour break for lunch. After the exam I was exhausted, hungry, and totally drained physically and mentally. Most of my classmates went out and celebrated, but I didn't. I stayed in alone, because I had no money.

Again, I went back to Mexico for a few more clinical rotations. I completed both obstetrics/gynecology and dermatology rotations. It was difficult without my family's support and money was scarce. I couldn't afford to buy any gifts from Mexico for my family; I was barely able to put gas in my car. Our school administrator told me that I would have to find another hospital to complete the rest of my clinical rotations in order to fulfill the rest of my clinical curriculum. This meant that I had to move again to another state.

Life had been hard enough and now I had to relocate again. "When is it going to end? I have no money!"

I recalled reading the Bible and learning that I can do all things through Christ who gives me strength.

I knelt down in my small studio apartment, with tears streaming down my cheeks, and prayed to God for a new path. Thoughts rushed through my mind and I could not sleep all night. The next day I drove to a local bookstore and started to browse the world travel section. I came across a tour guide book and as I flipped through the pages, the state of Alaska popped up. There were beautiful pictures of glaciers and mountaintops covered with snow, as well as the green landscape of the city of Anchorage.

I felt a voice coming from my conscious saying, "Go there and prosper."

I started to search for clinical rotations in Anchorage. I came across two hospitals that provided full medical services to the community—Alaska Native Medical Center and Providence Alaska Medical Center. I called both hospitals and asked for their medical clinical rotation department. I was told to leave my information and some-one would call me back. I waited patiently for two weeks and there was no response from either of the hospitals. I was worried and kept praying every day. I had a persistent feeling in my gut to call Alaska Native Medical Center. I picked up the phone and called. While the phone was ringing, waiting to be picked up, my heart pounded with apprehension and fear of rejection.

The phone was answered by a very pleasant female voice, "Hello, you have reached the Alaska Native Medical Center. This is the medical volunteer department. How may I help you?"

My voice was quivering and I said, "My name is Xa Xiong. I am a third-year medical student. I am seeking medical clinical rotation. I wonder if you offer any clinical rotation at your hospital."

The lady replied, "Do you have any specific clinical rotations that you are interested in?

I replied, "I am seeking surgical rotations."

She replied, "Yes, we do offer them for surgical residents but I'm not sure if we have any openings for medical students right now. Which medical school do you attend?"

I replied, "I attended Spartan Health Sciences University, School of Medicine in Saint Lucia Island in the Caribbean."

She replied, "Our medical students are usually from the state of Washington. I'm not sure if we accept medical students from other medical schools. But I will be happy to take a look at your resume if you can send it to me. Once I receive your resume and discuss this with our surgeons, I will let you know."

I gathered my resume, letter of recommendation and

transcript from my medical school, clinical rotation evaluations from Mexico and Arizona, and mailed them to her via FedEx.

Two weeks later, I received a phone call from the medical volunteer department of the Alaska Native Medical Center. "I have spoken to our surgeon, Dr. Francis Wilson, and she approved you starting your surgical rotation with her."

I was thrilled and thanked God for this wonderful opportunity. I called Choua and gave her the good news. She was not thrilled, but she understood.

She told me, "It's not like you are leaving for the military...you are only going to Alaska. We will be fine." I drove back home to Santa Ana and prepared for the long journey to Alaska. Our third daughter, Elena—meaning shining light—was born.

While home for such a short period of time, I tried to savor every moment to the fullest with Choua and the kids. The days and nights were quiet, with no news or phone calls from any of our close relatives, except my father-in-law, Chay Yia Yang; mother-in-law, Say Thao; and brother and sister-in-law, Mr. and Mrs. Zong Xia Yang. They were very supportive and encouraged us to pursue our dreams no matter how difficult it became.

My brother-in-law encouraged me with these inspiring words, "Set your heart into it and one day you will receive."

Despite the words of encouragement from my in-laws, I was still at one of the lowest points in my life where I had no money, low self-esteem, feelings of being discredited by others and profound uncertainty for the future. Choua and I were at one of the local book stores in the South Coast Plaza in Costa Mesa to strategize a plan to achieve our dreams. While we were browsing through the isle of the medicine section, we came across a book called *The Spirit Catches You and You Fall Down* by Anne Fadiman.[4] She captured the astounding events of a Hmong child who had severe epilepsy, American doctors, and the collision between two cultures. We bought the book with our credit card. I finished reading the book within a week. I was intrigued by the misunderstanding between the two different cultures that want the same result but have very different methods when providing care to an ill child. Both lacked understanding because the health care cultures clashed and ended in mistrust. I wanted to be the change and close the gap of the health care among our culture and the American culture. It energized me and made me even more determined to fulfill my dream of becoming a medical doctor despite the hardships.

The second book that influences me was *Gifted Hands* by Ben Carson, MD.[3] His personal story inspired me to pursue my medical career despite many obstacles to overcome. If he could start with nothing except ambition, then so could I.

Eventually, the time came and I packed my suitcases once again. My parents, Choua, and our kids drove me to LAX. It was time to say goodbye again. Tears streamed down our faces and in my heart I did not want to leave my family. They wished me the very best and asked God to protect me during my absence. The atmosphere was filled with the agony of separation and gloominess. I waved good-bye with sorrow in my heart. I didn't want to be alone again, but I had no choice. I had come too far to give it all up. After the long flight to Anchorage, I took a taxi from the airport to the Alaska Native Medical Center student housing apartment, which was only a five minutes' walk to the hospital.

Medical Rotations in Alaska

On the first day, I reported to the Alaska Native Medical Center (ANMC) volunteer department to complete the necessary forms as a training medical student. I was given an ID badge with my picture on it, labeled "Medical Student—Surgery." I was very excited! Housing and meals in the hospital cafeteria were complimentary. Having medical rotations in Alaska was astounding and the learning experience was phenomenal. Alaska was considered to be a third world country where medical training was practically all hands-on.

My attending physician, Dr. Francis Wilson, M.D., was one of the greatest surgeons I had ever known. She was not only a great mentor, but an excellent teacher with abundant experience and surgical knowledge. She allowed me to scrub for over eighty surgeries during the two-month rotation, usually as the first assistant.

She had me follow two other surgical residents, John and Patrick. They both were excellent surgical residents.

John was an easygoing senior surgical resident and loved to teach. He allowed me to be the first assistant in the majority of the cases.

Our surgical cases ranged from inserting a central line to cholecystectomy (removal of inflamed gallbladders either by surgery or laparoscopy), to skin grafts, to open abdominal surgeries. I literally lived in the hospital and slept in vacant patient rooms. I would ask the operator to page me first in response to calls or for emergency room surgical consultations. My two months' surgical rotation went by very quickly.

My final exam was placing a cardiac port for chemotherapy access with the assistance of my attending surgeon, Dr. Francis Wilson. The patient's surgery went very well with no complications. I was acknowledged for being one of the most "advanced improvement surgical students" by Dr. Wilson.

Eye, ear, nose, and throat (EENT) was another clinical rotation that I had the opportunity to take part in. There were several surgical cases I encountered that taught me to become a better diagnostic clinician. There was a young man who was snowmobiling and somehow flipped over his snowmobile. The medevac brought him in from one of the remote villages to our emergency room. I was paged to evaluate the patient. On his physical exam, he was alert and conversing with normal neurological findings, except I noticed a clear fluid that drained from both of his ears. I ordered a non-contrast head and cervical spine computer tomography (CT) scan with high probability of basilar skull fracture. His CT scan confirmed a simple linear fracture to the base of his skull. Luckily, surgical intervention was not indicated. I admitted him to the neurology floor with close monitoring. He did very well and sustained no focal neurological deficit. He survived and was discharged to go home on the second day. He was most thankful for being alive and reunited with his family.

Another case was a fourteen-year-old Alaskan native who attempted suicide after having an argument with her boyfriend and parents. She shot herself with a 9 mm under her chin. The bullet penetrated through her mouth, nose, and frontal lobe of the brain and then exited the skull. She was brought to the hospital, where we operated on her with a neurosurgeon for more than nine hours. She survived the incident and the operation. She was transferred to the University of Washington for critical care and facial plastic reconstruction. A few months later, she came back with a full facial reconstruction for follow-up. From these experiences, I became more determined to become a physician to save lives.

My final rotation was family practice in Nome where I spent two months with several excellent family physicians, providing medical care to Alaskan natives. My role was more as a senior resident since there was no medical resident at the time. Housing and meals were provided by the family medicine department at Norton Sound Regional Hospital. I lived and ate my meals in the hospital. On a daily routine, I started rounds with inpatients at 6 am by myself, and then followed my attending physicians at 8 am. I saw patients in the clinic and assisted with procedures in the afternoon. At night, I stayed in the hospital call room and covered both inpatient care and the emergency room. All kinds of ill patients came through the ER. Many of the cases involved alcoholics, trauma patients, and women in labor, as well as cases of frost bite.

One of the most memorable cases occurred early on Christmas morning, when a full-term pregnant woman came by ambulance to the emergency room leaking amniotic fluid. I was paged through my beeper and the overhead intercom to come to the emergency room. As I arrived in the ER, the ambulance pulled up to the front entry. An Alaskan native woman, who was in her early 30's, was pulled out of the back of the ambulance. She languished in pain with both hands guarding her belly. I rushed out to evaluate her while she was still on the stretcher. We wheeled her through the front door.

The pregnant lady exclaimed, "I feel like pushing!"

I responded, "Don't push yet! Wait until we get inside."

The pregnant lady exclaimed, "The baby is coming out now!!!"

I said, "Breathe, breathe, breathe…and don't push yet. We are almost there."

Once we arrived in the emergency room and she was transferred over to the ER bed, a brief medical history was obtained from the patient with no significant past medical history. A fetal monitor was placed over her abdomen. The fetal heart tone was 150 with regular uterine contractions every minute. There was no fetal distress noted on the fetal heart monitor. I proceeded with the physical examination. Her cervix was at 10 cm dilation. I turned around and called my attending physician. As I was talking to him over the phone the baby's head started to crown and came out without assistance. I hung up the phone and rushed over to the patient. Without any time to put on gloves or a gown, the infant was expelled completely. I caught the baby just in time with my bare hands. It was a boy! I began suctioning the baby's mouth so he wouldn't swallow the amniotic fluid. The baby took his very first breath and began to cry. The umbilical cord was clamped and cut with sterile scissors. He was wrapped in a new hospital sheet and placed over the top of the mother's chest. She cuddled the baby and started to cry. The mom was astounded that her son was born on Christmas day. The patient's placenta was delivered shortly after. She had no skin tears and had good homeostasis. Her vital signs were all within normal ranges, there was minimal blood loss, and there were no complications.

Both the mother and her newborn son did very well. They both were transferred to the obstetrics inpatient care ward.

The mother said, "Thank you for delivering my baby."

I called and notified my attending physician and he was very pleased with the delivery.

He told me, "I will see the mom and baby in the morning."

This was my very first delivery without supervision from an attending physician. The next day, my attending physician came in for rounds and I was given a great compliment.

Another exciting case took place around 4 am. An alcoholic man came in with a serious laceration. His wife had stabbed him in the back of his head over the occipital area with a fishing knife during a dispute. He sustained a deep skin laceration that was three inches long horizontally and bleeding profusely. A female officer escorted him with a dirty towel pressing against the laceration. Upon arrival in the ER, he was cuffed to the stretcher rail. The medical history was obtained through the patient and the officer. His laceration was explored and copiously flushed with saline irrigation solution. Local anesthetic with 2% Lidocaine was injected into the laceration site and the wound was further explored. The wound was deep enough to make his skull visible. Per his medical record, his last tetanus vaccination was ten years ago. Tetanus vaccine was given to him over the left deltoid area to prevent tetanus infection. His laceration was closed with multiple interrupted sutures. He was closely monitored for alcohol withdrawal throughout the morning and was discharged and escorted to jail on domestic abuse charges. What an exciting night!

I volunteered with the medevac team in Nome. We took calls from distant smaller villages to pick up critical patients and transport them to the main hospital in Anchorage by single-engine aircraft. There were times that we had to transport the patients through snowstorms. I had no fear of losing my life in a blizzard if we crushed, but my greatest fear was not being able to reach the patient in time to save the patient's life. It was fear-provoking but it was worth it—all the patients survived.

Shishmaref, Alaska

I was given the opportunity to travel to Shishmaref, a village on a small island about five miles from the mainland, to provide medical care. The island was only one mile across, and five hundred people lived there, mostly Alaskan natives. We traveled in a single-engine aircraft, with the pilot, one other physician assistant, a few native passengers, and myself. We packed the aircraft with food, drinks, canned food, and medical supplies.

Our aircraft had difficulty landing on the runway strip due to a blizzard with high winds. With many years of experience, the pilot was able to land the plane safely. We struggled through the snow and gusty winds to pack our things into a truck. We drove cautiously to the small clinic that consisted of a small waiting room, a receptionist's desk, three exam rooms, and a storage room in the back. The clinic was located adjacent to the cemetery. It looked very spooky to me, but to the villagers it was just another part of town.

During the winter, the visibility in Shishmaref was pretty dim, but it was possible to see other people. There were twenty hours of night and four hours of daylight with no sun visibility. On the first day we treated many patients with chronic diseases, several acute skin lacerations, and a few fractures which were medically manageable with splints.

I was pretty much on my own as a fourth year medical student and it was good medical practice. Fortunately, I did not have any deliveries to do, but I ended up doing a few sutures and splinting some fractures. The physician assistant had a shed where she would go to sleep and have a nice warm cup of cocoa. As for myself, I ended up sleeping inside the clinic's storage room. The room was very small and had a twin pull-up bed. I did not sleep well all night. On the second night, at one o'clock in the morning, I heard a noise pounding on the door. It terrified me. I jumped up and looked through the window. It was a man and a woman holding his hand with a white towel covered with blood.

I opened the door and asked, "What happened?"

The man replied, "I shot a polar bear a while ago...I was cutting the skin, somehow I sliced my hand. It was a big one."

I removed the towel and saw an enormous laceration across the palm of his left hand. The laceration was deep, in between the first and second fingers. The laceration was explored and I could see the injured tendons popping out. The laceration was still actively bleeding. I couldn't call the medevac to evacuate him to Nome or Anchorage due to the snowstorm. I did the best I could to clean his laceration and stop the bleeding. Lidocaine was injected into the laceration to create local anesthesia. Multiple interrupted sutures were used to repair the tendons and close the laceration. He tolerated the repair well with good homeostasis. The bleeding finally stopped. He was able to move all his fingers without any focal neurological deficit. Bacitracin (antibiotic) ointment applied to the suture site, covered with non-adhesive pad, and wrapped with kerlex dressing. The patient and his wife were very thankful and impressed with his laceration repair. I asked him to come back in the morning for a recheck. He and his wife came back to the clinic later in the morning and brought in a bowl of polar bear stew and offered it to me. I never had polar bear meat before, but it smelled really good. I couldn't resist, so I accepted their gift. I was very thankful to the couple for feeding me.

We were scheduled to fly back to Nome on the third day; however our plane could not land due to the blizzard. We ended up extending our stay at Shishmaref for a few more days until the snowstorm cleared. Each day we listened to our radio radar but there was no good news. We were told continuously that the plane could not land. Soon we had been on the island for seven days. I ended up eating most of the canned food in the storage room. I believe I gave medical care to over a hundred patients in those seven days. It gave me the opportunity to learn and practice as a real doctor in a rural setting, where you need to provide medical care to the patient with whatever you have.

One day, I took a walk through the middle of the town. It was very windy and the visibility was very poor. I stopped at a little shop in the middle of the town. There were a lot of old antiques that had been around for hundreds of years. I had a strong feeling inside my heart, but I didn't know what it was. An elderly lady, probably in her nineties or maybe even a hundred years old, came out from the back room and showed me a green stone jewel. She told me it was from an ancient axe that she had kept for many years.

She said, "It will bring you good luck and prosperity."

She offered it to me for the price of five hundred dollars. I told her I was just a medical student and I didn't have much money. So she said she could sell it to me for two hundred dollars. I looked at her and realized she probably needed the money more than I did. I ended up charging it on my credit card. It was a piece of art, a gift, and an antique that has been around for over hundreds or thousands of years. Before I left the store, the elderly lady blessed the stone jewel for good health, good wealth, much prosperity, and success in my education. I thanked her for her blessing and words of wisdom.

That Sunday afternoon, the snowstorm suddenly cleared, and our aircraft was able to land. We immediately got into the aircraft. I looked back and saw many people waving good-bye. I could see the glimmer in their eyes saying thank you. We left Shishmaref and came back to Nome safely, where I completed the rest of my family practice rotation.

Finally, a Medical Doctor (M.D.)

During the week of February, 2000, I gathered my belongings and got on the airplane in Nome and flew back to the Ted Stevens Anchorage International Airport, where I took a connecting flight to Los Angeles. I felt closer to home as our plane approached the airport. Finally, it landed.

I said to myself, "No more temperatures below zero

and no more blizzards"

As I came through the corridor gate door, I saw Choua, our kids, and my parents anxiously waiting. As soon as they saw me, Elizabeth, Einstein, Emily and Elena ran over to hug me. I, of course, cried tears of joy. Everyone felt at ease when I was home again.

I was happy to be back and to finally have fulfilled my clinical rotation requirements. I submitted all my evaluations to the Spartan Health Sciences University, School of Medicine administrators and waited anxiously for the results. After an extensive review by the administrators and our school dean, finally I was approved to receive my MD degree. My diploma was conferred on April 21, 2000.

My student loans in both chiropractic and medical schools totaled over $120,000. We were financially broke. We started to receive loan repayment statements from the loan agency. I couldn't sleep and kept having nightmares how we were going to repay the loans. The saddest part was that no one really knew how much we struggled financially. No one called to say congratulations or dropped by to check how we were doing.

I even heard several close relatives doubting us and saying, "Graduating from a foreign medical school with an MD degree will not guarantee a residency program in the United States. He wasted his time and money."

Our usually optimistic spirits were totally distraught. Choua and I were heartbroken. We drove to my old school—Concordia University (previously known as Christ College Irvine). We both knelt down in front of "The Good

Shepherd" statue again and prayed, asking for new direction and for open doors to help me pass the United States Medical Licensing Examination (USMLE) and to be accepted to a family medicine residency program. In addition, we asked God to show us the next chapter in our lives and to give us the guidance we needed to succeed. We promised God that we would do whatever he had in store for our future.

It appeared that our prayer was not answered soon enough. I started to worry and panic. We didn't have enough money to keep us going on a monthly basis. Choua was the only one who was working at the time, earning only eight dollars per hour. We ran out of student loan money and we struggled. There were many times when people had celebrations, birthday parties, ceremonies, and we were not invited. Later on we found out that people were speculating that we were poor and did not have enough money to give or to buy a gift for the special occasion. That was the reason why we were never invited.

Occasionally, Choua would hear people say to our kids, "If you were my kids, I would buy you new clothes."

Sadly, we had promised our kids many times that we would buy them new clothes, but had not been able to do so. We were broke, barely making enough to pay our rent, car payments, and credit cards. Our credit cards were maxed. The only thing between us and the homeless people down the street was that we had a home to live in but they did not. Choua and I sat and discussed what our future would bring if I did not go to work and unable to get into residency. What would our life be? Choua was my encouragement.

She said to me, "Put your heart into it, you can do it. Even though we have to suffer now, think about years from now. You will become someone. If you don't pursue it now, in ten years we'll still be poor."

Deep down inside, I did not want to fail Choua and my children. I started to pick up the books again and study for the USMLE. I decided to go down to Houston, Texas, for a Kaplan review course in preparation for the exam. It appeared that traveling would never end for me. Again, I had to pack up my suitcases, and leave my children behind, as well as my parents and my wife. I started to feel depressed again. Nevertheless, there was no other choice except to move on. I took a flight to Houston, and went to Kaplan Center and registered my name. I looked for a place to live within the area. Thankfully, I found someone who was also enrolled in the board review program to share an apartment with. He had rented a two-bedroom apartment and was looking for a roommate. Neither one of us had a car. We walked thirty minutes each way from our apartment to the Kaplan Center. It was humid and hot but we had to make the sacrifice to learn and study for our exam.

A Close Call

I was under a lot of stress during my studies. Four weeks into the board review course, I started to experience major abdominal pain. I bought antacid medications over the counter and started taking them faithfully. One day my symptoms began to worsen, and I fainted as we were on the bus going downtown. It was hot, sunny, and I thought the sickness was related to dehydration. I drank lot of water and felt slightly better. However, in the evening, I started to have nausea, vomiting black contents, severe abdominal pain, and black tarry stool diarrhea. I felt very weak and fatigued but experienced no chest pain. Choua and I did not have health insurance at that time so I resisted going to the emergency room. I was too weak to make a phone call to my family. My roommate ended up calling my wife. I told my wife over the phone that my stool was black and I was getting very tired and weak. She told me to go to the emergency room. I was reluctant because it would cost a fortune to go to the ER. I spoke to my mother.

She said, "You have to go to the ER, Son. There's not much we can do being so far away from you, but you need to go to the hospital and get a checkup."

I was still contemplating what to do when Choua got on the phone and demanded, "Go to the emergency room now!" She also spoke to my roommate and told him, "Whatever the cost is, we will pay for it, but please take my husband to the emergency room!"

My roommate called a cab and fifteen minutes later, the cab arrived to take me to the ER. It took me a while to get downstairs even with the help of my roommate. The cab took us directly to West Houston Medical Center emergency room. Upon arrival, the nurses rushed to our cab and put me in a wheelchair. They wheeled me into the emergency room. The ER Physician examined me immediately. An electrocardiogram (ECG) was performed and labs were drawn. I was supplemented with oxygen per nasal cannula. Bolus intravenous fluid was given rapidly. The ER physician told me that my ECG was normal and there was no sign of heart attack. It was a relief. About ten minutes later, I had an episode of severe cramping abdominal pain and I asked to use the bathroom. The nurse dragged along all of the IV poles and IV fluid with me to the bathroom. After I used the bathroom, I stood up, stumbled and fell onto the floor because I was too weak to walk. I managed to push the red emergency light in the bathroom. The nurses rushed in and pulled me off the ground and took me to the gurney. The emergency doctor rushed in and told me that I had severe internal bleeding. My hemoglobin was down to 4 (normal 12 to 14) and I would need a massive blood transfusion. He would need to admit me into the intensive care unit and start a blood transfusion immediately. I asked him if I could be admitted to the regular medical floor. He asked me why, and I told him I did not have health insurance and it would be very costly for me to pay for it.

He told me, "If you don't get well, who's going to pay your bill?"

In other words, if he did not admit me to the intensive care unit and gave me blood transfusion, I would die. Without further hesitation, I was wheeled to the ICU for intravenous fluid, medication, and blood transfusion with close monitoring.

After four packs of red blood cell transfusions, I

started to feel better and gained some energy back, but I was still having black tarry stools. The ICU physician consulted with the gastroenterologist. He came in my room and said I may have upper gastrointestinal bleeding. He further recommended an upper endoscopy (a nonsurgical procedure using a flexible tube with light and camera to examine the digestive tract) to look for the source of bleeding in my stomach. He explained the risk of the procedure including esophageal and stomach perforation and even death. I was alone with no one by my side. I thought to myself what would happen if I died during the procedure. My wife and kids would not have a husband or father. The GI doctor told me that I would have an excellent chance of survival if I chose to have the procedure done. I took the chance and signed the consent form for the procedure. He gave a sedative medication through my intravenous line. As soon as I felt the warmth in my arm I was completely out. Thirty minutes after the procedure, I started to arouse. The gastroenterologist told me he found a large stomach ulcer the size of a dime that was oozing blood, and he had cauterized the ulcer with a burner so the bleeding could stop.

The doctor said, "Everything went smoothly and there were no further complications."

I was fortunate to survive. My hemoglobin and hematocrit levels started to rise again. I regained my strength and began to eat normal food on day two. I was depressed because I was all alone. Choua, my children and my parents were all in California.

I started to realize, "What am I doing here? I should be

with my family. If I die here, no one will even see me."

At that moment, I started to pray to God. After my prayer, I could sense God watching over me. He did not let me die. He wanted me to understand how valuable life was so that when I recuperated, I could dedicate myself to helping others to get well. There was a Bible next to the bed and I started reading the book of Genesis. It gave me the strength to stay healthy physically, psychologically, and spiritually. It also gave me the strength to fulfill my dreams. I recalled the footprint dream, where a troubled man looked back on the sand and saw only one set of footprints. He asked God why there was only one set of footprints when he was suffering. God responded to him that he was being carried in His arms. That reminded me that God was carrying me through my suffering moments. I was no longer afraid of being alone.

On the third day, I felt great! I no longer had abdominal pain or black tarry stools. I felt like a new person, more determined than ever. I asked to leave because of financial difficulty. They discharged me with antibiotics and antacid medications. I thanked God again for extending my life. I went back to the Kaplan review course, completed the rest of the learning sessions and flew back to California. I was blessed to see Choua, my children and my parents again. There I thrived! Our son, Alexander—named after the Ancient Greek King, Alexander the Great—was born.

A Clinic in Louisiana

I was glad to be home with my family in Santa Ana, but my long journey of medical practice was still a work in progress. I continued to review day and night for the United States Medical Licensing Examination. I was jobless and Choua was only bringing in nine dollars per hour. Choua's income was mainly used for paying our mortgage, cars, and car insurance. We had very little money for food, clothing, and spending money. We had not bought any new clothes or shoes for ourselves or the kids for quite a while.

One day we drove by Newport Beach on HWY 101 along the coast of Orange County and saw many enormous houses facing the ocean with multiple luxury cars parked in the driveways. We could only dream of having one, and our dream seemed very distant.

I told Choua that someone said, "There is a light at the end of the tunnel."

She wondered when we would reach the light at the end of our tunnel.

We passed a 1996 blue Lamborghini Sport 2-door sedan.

I told Choua, "I could only dream of having that car."

Choua responded, "You will, one day."

Choua and I kept praying and placed our future life in God's hands. Our prayers were answered. When I was doing my clinical rotations in Alaska, I met an urologist who was my attending physician. Unexpectedly, I received a phone call from him stating that he would be moving to

Leesville, Louisiana to start a urology clinic and wanted to know if I would work for him. He proposed to pay me $40,000 a year. I accepted the position and broke the good news to Choua. It was God's blessing for us. It meant, however, I had to leave the family again. I packed all my necessary belongings in our 1995 Isuzu Rodeo. The hardest part of leaving involved the emotional distress again, but this time my parents went along with me.

We drove all night from Santa Ana, across the deserts of Arizona to Texas, and finally arrived in Leesville, Louisiana. It took us twenty-eight hours to reach our destination. During the course of the drive, I had the opportunity to talk to my parents. The conversations about both of my parents' lives were recorded. There were many stories told during the night to keep us awake.

My father repeatedly said, "Education is very important in life...And in this world, the greatest gift is LOVE."

He wanted me to finish my medical doctor degree and residency program, and most importantly, be a leader within the community. Then, our family would be considered prosperous. My father's heart was for me to be successful. He wished me the very best in my medical education.

He told me, "One day you will become a great leader...a leader that will help people from the bottom of your heart without a profit-making purpose."

I always kept my father's words. We made it to Leesville. Although, we didn't have money to eat in a fancy restaurant, we did get to try some alligator meat at a local family restaurant with reasonable prices. The next day, my parents departed back to Santa Ana. I remained behind to work as an urologist assistant. My first paycheck was about $3,500. That was the most money I had ever made in one month of my life! I sent most of the money to Choua and my parents. We were able to pay for our car, house and credit cards, and we were even able to buy some gifts for my parents and kids.

The second month the practice did not go as I expected, so I packed my belongings into my 1995 Rodeo and drove back to California. I was happy to be home with my family again but with much resentment in my heart.

California Again and Finally Wisconsin

A few months after I came back from Leesville, we were broke again. No money! There was only worry and anxiety in the house. I started to doubt myself and was losing my self-esteem and the respect of my community. Life did not seem to be turning out the way I expected. I kept praying to God. There were multiple times that we were financially unstable and filled with distress. We continued to kneel down in front of the Good Shepherd statue at Concordia University and pray. There was no answer. The wind remained still and silent. Suddenly we received an invoice from the West Houston Medical Center for the amount of $10,000 for which we only had 30 days to pay. I was not working. We were ultimately broke and could barely afford to pay our mortgage, bills, and to put food on the table. We didn't pay the bill and it was sent to a collection agency. I received several letters from the collection agency stating that if we didn't pay the bill, our credit score would be jeopardized. The collection agency constantly called but we were afraid to pick up the phone. One day, I was irritated by the ringing phone and I started to dispute with the collection agency. I told them that I did not have the money to pay for the bill. Ultimately, the collection agency and I came to an agreement. The collection agency began to work with the fees and told me that if I could pay $4,000 in cash, they would wipe out the other $6,000. I didn't have enough money, so my parents pitched in $2,000. I still owed the other $2,000. Fortunately, Choua had saved $2,000 before we got married, and even though it was never meant to be spent, we had no option. We combined our money with my parents' $2,000 to pay for my medical bill. The weight of this debt was lifted off our shoulders, but now we were more desperate than ever.

I started talking to Choua again and told her I needed to finish my medical board exams, otherwise we would go nowhere. She was tired of hearing about me going away again, but I told her this would be the last time. I would study hard and pass the board exams so I could apply for residency. Choua agreed, so I packed up my suitcases again and drove back to Houston. I stayed there for six months, eating and breathing my books. I did everything I possibly could. I finished the course review and told myself I would not go back to California until I passed my medical board. I wanted to find a different place where I could be successful. I told Choua and my parents that I wanted to go to

Wisconsin. It was a hard decision but Choua was agreeable to it as were my parents. I started to pack my suitcases and I had my brother-in-law fly from Milwaukee, Wisconsin, to Houston. I picked him up at the airport and we started driving to Wisconsin. We made the trip without any problems. I ended up maxing out all my credit cards along the way.

I stayed with my sister and brother-in-law in Milwaukee for a few months. I was broke and had no money in my pockets. I drove to St. Paul, Minnesota to search for a job. The trip was unsuccessful. There was no hiring at the time so I ended up coming back to Milwaukee, where I found a job working as a medical assistant at one of the local pain clinics. I worked there for a month, but it did not go too well; there was a lawsuit against the physician, so I started to look for another job. I kept praying to God, asking him to give me a position where I could improve myself and help people the way God intended. As I was sending out applications, there was a clinician position open at the Kajsiab House in Madison, Wisconsin, which was under the umbrella of the Dane County Mental Health Center. With my MD degree, I was fully qualified for the position. A few days after I submitted my application, I received a phone call from human resources saying that they would like to schedule an interview. I was thrilled and I thanked God that finally something was happening. I went to the interview and everything went well. I was offered the clinician position. The job was in Madison, but at the time I was living in Milwaukee. It was quite a distance that I had to drive every day. Nevertheless, I was willing to take the risk. I talked to Choua and my parents in California about bringing my family to Wisconsin. At first, they hesitated, but it was best for us to be together.

In December 2003, my family finally moved to Wisconsin, but my parents and my younger brother with his wife and children remained in California. At last Choua, the children and I were reunited. We rented a small cozy three-bedroom apartment in Milwaukee, and I drove to Madison for my job every day.

I worked at the Kajsiab House, where I performed counseling and managed client's cases. I had the opportunity to work with two of the most influential providers who worked diligently with the Southeast Asian population in the state of Wisconsin, Dr. Fred Coleman, MD—Psychiatrist— and Dr. Roger Garms, PhD—Psychologist. They both were excellent mentors and taught me well. God sent me there. I was able to touch a lot of hearts and was able to help the patients get well because of my medical background and fluency in both English and Hmong languages. I also had the opportunity to work with a Tai Chi master to develop a Hmong exercise. I spent many hours counseling the patients and coordinating the Hmong exercises inspired by daily chores the Hmong people had been performing way back in Laos, such as chopping wood, grinding rice, pounding rice, and plowing rice.

While I was making very little money, I was able to take the time off to complete my USMLE Step 2 exam. I spent many hours studying and doing thousands of practice board questions. I took the exam and succeeded! I started seeking the Family Medicine Residency Program. As a foreign medical graduate, my chances of finding a matching program in Wisconsin were very slim. I applied at the University of Wisconsin Family Medicine Residency Programs in Madison and Appleton with much fear. Both programs were extremely competitive. We prayed daily, asking God for direction. In the middle of applying to the family medicine residency program, I received unexpected news. The State newspaper contacted my workplace. They wanted to feature my life in a cover story. On August 9th, 2004 my picture appeared on the front page of The Wisconsin Sentinel with the title, "Physician Ministers to the Hmong," by Susan Lampert Smith. I sent the newspaper to my father and mother in California. My parents were thrilled to see me on the front page of the newspaper. They were very proud of me. My father would take the newspaper with him to show all of the nurses during his dialysis.

My father called me and told me over the phone, "We'll have a big party to celebrate your success once you have been accepted to the residency program." I kept his words in my heart.

Receiving Bad News

Several months went by after submitting my application through the National Residency Matching Program (NRMP) for the University of Wisconsin Family Medicine Residency Program in Madison and the University of

Wisconsin Fox Valley in Appleton. Choua and I waited anxiously to hear from the residency programs. Life was silent and my future was motionless. I couldn't sleep; thoughts raced through my head each night. One morning in October 2004, I was at my desk at work and heard my cell phone ring. I answered and it was my mom. She started to cry immediately.

I asked my mom, "What is wrong and why are you crying?"

She continued to sob without saying a word. My heart started to beat faster and faster as though something had gone wrong. I kept asking my mom to tell me what was going on.

She took a short breath and stuttered, "Your—your dad just had a stroke during his dialysis."

I responded, "What...are you sure?"

She said, "Yes! The nurse has called the ambulance and he is on his way to the emergency room."

I broke down in tears. My body went into shock. Numbness engulfed my entire body. I got down on my knees and started praying for my dad and my mom. I called Choua and told her the bad news. She was also in shock and no words left her lips. I immediately got on the next flight to the John Wayne Orange County Airport in Santa Ana. While I was in the air, I kept praying for my father and begged God to restore his physical health. The air remained as silent as the desert below me. As soon as I arrived I went directly to the hospital where my father was. I opened the door and saw my mother and brother sitting next to my dad.

The sound of the nurses and doctors were muted and all I could hear was the rhythmic breathing of my father's ventilation machine taped to his mouth.

He was on one hundred percent life support. His eyes were closed and unresponsive. My mom was sitting next to my dad holding his hand, with tears streaming down her face. The wrinkles on her eyes were strained and her teeth chattered repeatedly. I held her in my arms and we cried together. I tried every possible way to speak to my dad but he only replied with silence.

My father's doctor walked in and told us, "I'm sorry. Your dad had a hemorrhagic stroke in his brain stem. There is not much we can do, except give your dad time for the next seventy-two hours. We should know by then if he is going to make it or not."

It was not what I wanted to hear but it was the fact. I stayed and watched my dad with endless tears and sadness in my heart. There was nothing I could do. No matter how much I knew about medicine, I couldn't save him.

I questioned God, "Why are you doing this to me. You took my brother and my sister. And now, you are going to take my dad away from me too? Why? Why? Why, God?"

There was no answer. The room filled with silence. As I watched my father lying quietly on the hospital bed I broke down and cried with the hope that God would restore him to his normal state of health.

Hours went by and my father remained unresponsive. The doctor visited my dad early in the morning and reported that his most recent MRI showed no worsening of his hemorrhagic stroke but since his stroke was so massive he would not recover as expected. The doctor proposed a feeding tube and a tracheostomy placement for long-term life support with a ventilation machine. The entire family had a long discussion and we all consented to it. My dad's illness continued to deteriorate despite doing everything the doctor suggested. He was transferred to a skilled nursing home. After his move, I came home to Madison. We kept my father in our prayers every day in the hopes that God would restore his health. Days and nights were filled with silence.

A few weeks later, I was at work and my cell phone rang. It was my brother. Even before I could answered the phone, I felt a jolt in my heart and the numbness shot through my body I knew right away that something was wrong.

My brother said, "They have transferred dad to the hospital and he doesn't look good. You better come."

I instantly fell down onto my knees and started praying. I asked God to watch over my father and to sustain his life so I could see him. I left work immediately and got on the very first flight to Santa Ana. Two hours after my plane took off, at thirty-four thousand feet; my dad took his last breath. Below me was a bed of clouds and around me was the blue atmosphere near the stars. Little did I know, this would be his new home.

When I arrived at the hospital he was sleeping comfortably with no breathing tube in his mouth. A wave of emotions engulfed my body and as I exhaled, tears falling uncontrollably. I held him tightly to my chest and tried to wake him from his deep slumber, but his eyes remained closed. He had already gone to live with the Lord.

My mom was at home when my dad passed. As her son, I knew it would be difficult to tell her that her husband had died. I drove to my parent's home.

I held my mom and told her, "Dad left us behind." She broke down in tears for the longest time.

My dad's funeral was held in Santa Ana. Everyone remembered him as a man of great integrity, a loving husband, a wonderful father, a caring grandfather, a truly patriotic man, a prodigious and benevolent leader who provided service with charitable kindness rather than for personal profit. He was buried at the Eternal Valley Memorial Park in Newhall, California.

My father's last words to the world were, "The greatest gift is LOVE."

Receiving Good News

One month after my father's funeral, I received my interview invitations in the mail from both the University of Wisconsin Family Medicine Residency Program in Madison and the University of Wisconsin Fox Valley in Appleton. My family and I were very happy but saddened at the same time. My dad was not there to see my interview letters. I went to my interview without him this time, but I felt his presence all around me. I wished my father was there with me physically but I knew deep down in my heart he was with me spiritually. Both residency programs were excellent and the interview went very well. Since we were living in Madison at the time, completing my Family Medicine Residency in Madison would make more sense than in Appleton. We kept praying, telling God we would follow his guidance wherever he wanted us to go. We waited anxiously for the National Resident Matching Program (NRMP) Match Day to arrive.

The NRMP Match Day arrived on March 17, 2005. Susan Lampert Smith from the Wisconsin State Sentinel newspaper returned with her photographer to do a follow up interview on my story. Choua, several of my co-workers and I were all sitting in my office as I was about to open the National Residency Matching Program online. I wished my dad and my mom were with us. My heart was pounding so fast; it was about to burst out of my chest. I kept asking myself what would happen if I did not get a match. All the hard work I had invested would go down the drain. Choua was very confident and reassuring that I would match. I was trembling, and could barely think clearly. Watching and hearing the clock ticking, my heart was even more thunderous. The time arrived with great nervousness. I embraced the mouse in my hand with my index finger on the clicking button. I clicked on the matching icon on the website. I stared at the screen with intensity and the entire room was so silent I could feel the thickness in the air. A box popped up on the screen and indicated that I was successfully matched with the Fox Valley Family Medicine Residency Program.

The thick and depressing air in the room suddenly escaped through my office and the heavy weight bearing down on our shoulders lifted. What a huge relief! I was excited, along with my wife and co-workers. Choua gave me a big hug and the newspaper photographer took a snapshot of that moment. It was a joyful special day for my family and me. All the hard work and studying finally paid off. I called my mom in California and gave her the good news. I thanked her for everything she had done for me. She was filled with joy and broke down with happy tears! My story was featured on the front page of the Wisconsin State Sentinel—"Medical Residency is Fruition of Refugee Camp Promise."

Afterwards, I knelt down in one of the local churches and prayed to God and to my father, thanking them for being a part of my life. It was heartbreaking at the same time, because my father was not able to share this great moment with me. Tears ran down my cheeks. No matter how hard I tried to stop them, I couldn't. My father was a vital part in my life. He was my inspiration. Had he been here to see this day, he would be so proud and jubilant. All I could do was pray to him and thank him for everything.

CHAPTER NINE

Achieving the Impossible Dream

Kajsiab House

We lived in Madison, where I worked as a clinician at the Kajsiab House. The word Kajsiab in Hmong means free of stress or tension. The Kajsiab House was developed to serve the Hmong elders and their families in Dane County by providing social services to increase the understanding and the ability to adapt within the American culture as well as receive treatment for mental health conditions. When I announced my resignation to pursue my family medicine residency in Appleton, the staff and participants at the Kajsiab House were saddened, but they supported my decision. Everyone wanted to have a farewell party celebrating the success of my new medical endeavor. When the staff and elders at the Kajsiab House discussed the party arrangements, Choua and I were financially worried. Amazingly, the staff and elders were very supportive and offered to take full responsibility of the cooking and performing the celebration ceremony. A dream was fulfilled when Dr. Fred Coleman, MD, offered to purchase a cow for a thousand dollars to celebrate the event. A whole cow! What a relief! Dr. Fred

Coleman was truly a good man, and I learned so much from his experiences and guidance. Typically in the Hmong culture, the parents or close relatives were responsible for leading and financially supporting the celebration such as this one. Unfortunately, I was fatherless and did not have close relatives to host such a grand event. My mother was not able to attend because she was still living in California and we didn't have enough money to purchase a plane ticket for her to come. As we celebrated, my eyes began to tear. I could feel my father's spirit among us and the happiness he had always longed for. The elders and the staff gave many blessings. They all wished us the very best of luck, good health, and prosperity as we journeyed through the next phase of our lives. My wife and I were most thankful to everyone for their love and support.

A New Home in Appleton

In June 2005, we drove to Appleton to find a temporary place for me to live while doing my residency. We were able to afford a small, two-bedroom apartment on the west side of Appleton with no air-conditioning. The lease was six hundred dollars a month and we signed a contract for one year. I moved a few pieces of furniture from home into the apartment, while Choua and the children remained in Madison. The vicious cycle of separation occurred again but this time, I would only be two hours away. Before my drive to Appleton, I gave my family the usual departing hug and long goodbye. No matter how many times I had to leave my family, it never got easier. When I arrived at my new apartment in Appleton, the loneliness crept in and the separation anxiety returned once again. I was better prepared this time and told myself, "I worked so hard to get here, I have to keep going and make my family proud."

In July 2005, the Family Residency Program at Fox Valley Family Medicine finally began. The night before the big day, I was very anxious but excited to enter the hospital world as a Medical Resident. I envisioned myself wearing my surgical scrub with a doctoral white coat, a stethoscope around my neck, walking down the hospital hall and being paged, "Dr. Xiong, please come to the OR. Dr. Xiong, please come to the ER. Dr. Xiong, please come to ICU." Eventually, the alarm clock woke me up at 6 am.

I showered, put on my scrubs, and my doctor's white coat. Orientation was due to start at eight o'clock, but I arrived at the clinic around seven-thirty. I strolled around and got myself oriented with the place. I met five of my colleagues and chatted with them for a while. Our residency orientation lasted about two weeks, introducing us to our patient care, salary, rotation schedules, and hospital credentials. I completed all the necessary documentation and fulfilled certification for the Advance Cardiac Life Support and Neonatal Resuscitation Program (NRP). I was introduced to the hospital programs at Appleton Medical Center and St. Elizabeth's Hospital where most of my rotations would take place. I was excited but at the same time nervous and afraid to see my first patient.

At first, it was only a dream, but in a few days I was

seeing patients whose lives depended on me. It was nerve-wracking, but I was motivated and excited about reaching my dream.

First Medical Rotation as a M.D. Resident

My first rotation was internal medicine at the Appleton Medical Center (AMC). A typical day started at 6 am and ended at 6 pm. I would have to be in the hospital at least half an hour prior to the starting time. Routinely, the mornings began with patient rounds with either the senior resident physician or the junior resident physician. The patients were divided equally among the senior resident physician and the junior resident physician. The junior resident physician would take on new patients daily. Ten patients were assigned to me with the additional new admissions. At 6:30 am, I started to see my assigned patients. The goal was to see every patient before 10 am. On a routine round, I would see each of my assigned patients, perform an exam, review test results (both blood and diagnostic testing) and write a treatment plan with new orders.

When I reached my second patient, I was paged to go down to the emergency room to admit a patient. I responded to the page and told the nurse that I would be down in the ER in about ten to fifteen minutes. As I finished seeing my second patient, I rushed down to the ER and performed a history and physical exam on an elderly female patient with congestive heart failure. A brief admission note was written on the patient's chart with a plan of treatment and order for cardiology consultation. The patient's history, physical examination and plan of care were dictated. The patient was admitted to the medical floor for care.

I continued my rounds with constant interruptions from the nurses, attending physicians, new admissions and discharged patients. Time flew by and it was close to 5:30 pm. The night shift resident physician had already arrived. By the time I made all my rounds and handed my charts to him, it was already 6:30 pm. I left for home and started over again on the next day.

During the first month of my residency, the Post-Crescent newspaper reporter requested to do a cover story on me. I consented to it and a documentary story called "Rookie Docs" was featured on the front page.

At times I was tired, exhausted and ready to quit. There were close to a thousand times I told myself to give up and work a normal job just like everyone else. But each time I thought about quitting, I would hear Pastor Joel Osteen's voice echoing in my conscious mind, "Keep pressing forward and you shall receive."

I kept reminding myself that I had spent nearly twenty years of my life preparing for this moment and even when I had been closed to death, I did not quit. I continued to work hard night and day, spending many hours reading medical literature, practicing surgical techniques and keeping up with the latest medical treatments and medications.

The attending physicians would question the resident physicians in regard to patient care. For example, what was the diagnosis(s), the treatment plan(s), and how soon could the patient could be discharged? Typically, the attending physician would take full responsibility of their patients, but as a paid resident, we had to know what we were doing, otherwise the responsibility and the liability could fall onto us completely. I spent many hours in the hospital. Although I finished my rotation, I knew I would have to be back the following morning, following up and keeping updates on each of the assigned patients. There were many moments when I was tired and exhausted, but I reminded myself to keep going, that it was only three years before I would become a full-fledged medical doctor.

We had grand rounds on a weekly basis that involved case study presentations for certain patients, which was nerve-wracking. This opened up discussion and your colleagues, attending physicians, or the program director could ask any question regarding the patient's condition and the management founded on evidence-based practice. I had to prepare well and answer the questions appropriately. This required time and effort to master the materials.

There were many occasions when I was paged to the intensive care unit to pronounce someone dead. It was difficult in the beginning, but after many experiences, it became more comfortable. Confirming a patient's death was the easy part; telling the patient's family was the harder thing to do.

Obstetrics and gynecology was another interesting rotation that I encountered at St. Elizabeth Hospital. We had two resident shifts. The first shift covered 6 am to 6 pm. The second shift covered 6 pm to 6 the next morning. We had a busy obstetrics ward. I was constantly admitting patients and called in for deliveries. One night, I was called to evaluate a patient. Her cervical dilation was at ten centimeters and the baby's head starting descending rapidly. I paged the attending physician and he was on his way in. The patient went into delivery immediately. I didn't have time to put on a gown. I had my scrubs on, but there was no time to put gloves on. The baby expelled from the birth canal suddenly. I caught the newborn just in time in my bare hands. The newborn was cleaned the umbilical cord was clamped and cut, and the newborn was placed on an infant warmer. The placenta was delivered shortly without difficulty, and the patient had good hemostasis. However, she sustained a second-degree tear, which had to be repaired. By the time I started the repair, the attending physician came through the door.

He told me, "So, you delivered the baby."

I responded, "Yes!"

He replied, "Great job! You don't need me to be here."

I told him to wait, that I did need him to be present for legal reasons. We chuckled and laughed after we left the room. After that experience, my confidence in delivering babies was off the charts. I fully enjoyed it, and continued to deliver babies and manage prenatal care at the clinic. Time went by so quickly. I finished my first year of residency and went onto the second.

Before I knew it, the third year was approaching. I continued to provide medical care to my patients in our residency clinic along with our walk-in clinic and hospitals. We had an outstanding nursing home rotation at Brewster Valley where I spent three months caring for the geriatric patients. I loved working with the elderly and the newborn. To understand the complexity of the elderly, I had to have patience and dedication. I was glad that I came prepared with the passion to work with the elderly patients, and I was able to provide excellent care for their physical, mental, and spiritual needs. As a family physician, I needed to develop a good relationship with my patients, especially the elderly, otherwise they will not trust me, nor want me to be their doctor. The key thing was to be a diligent provider, have abundant patience, be a good listener, and build a good friendship with the patients. I was well prepared to serve them.

During my three years as a resident, I spent many hours helping the Hmong community and my Hmong patients. During that time, the 2007 Legal Act was enforced for disabled non-US citizens. If an individual had not received his or her US Citizenship within five years of residing in United States, the government's financial assistance was discontinued. Many people were over-whelmingly worried and distressed. In order for them to be waived from the United States Citizenship examination, they needed to complete Form N-648—Medical Certification for Disability Exceptions. This form would have to be signed by a licensed medical doctor or a psychologist willing to state that their disability or impairment would cause lifelong intellectual disability and prevent him or her from demonstrating knowledge and understanding of English and/or civics. These individuals were born in Laos and had minimal to no education. They were survivors from the Vietnam War and many suffered posttraumatic stress disorder, generalized anxiety, and major depression disorder. The individuals developed sleep disturbances and persistent intrusive emotional thoughts which resulted in poor concentration, memory problems, and learning incapability. My clinic began to fill up with Hmong and Laotian patients. They came to see me for a period of time based on their medical and mental health conditions. I completed the Form N-648 to exempt them from taking both the oral and written exams. Then they received their US Citizenship. The number of patients whom I helped was countless. I had several patients whose government financial support was discontinued but I was able to help them obtain their citizenship and reinstate their government funding. They were very thankful for my professional support and assistance.

In addition, I helped bridge the gaps in the healthcare systems in the cities of Appleton, Green Bay, Oshkosh, and Manitowoc. I conducted many healthcare conferences to make the Hmong population understand the healthcare system of the United States, as well as raise Hmong culture awareness to health care providers so they could provide services to accommodate the Hmong people. Many lives were saved, and many misunderstandings were resolved. Tension between the City of Appleton and the medical care system was relieved. Providers were able to give culturally appropriate services and became more understanding of the Hmong. Patients became more compliant to medication intake, appointments, and follow up with medical specialists and more agreeable to surgery. The Hmong community became healthier. What an honor it was to be part of this accomplishment.

Awarding Medical Licensure

When I submitted my application for my medical licensure, I was informed that I had to go in for an oral interview before the Medical Examining Board so they could determine my credentials. It was hard enough to pass all the United States Medical Licensing Examinations and finish residency training; now I had to face the Medical Examining Board for an interview.

"When is this going to end?" I said to myself.

The interview was scheduled, and Choua encouraged me that it would be all right. We went down to Madison and sat in a long line with other physicians who were also waiting for their oral interview. My palms were sweating and my heart was throbbing with nervousness.

Finally, it was my turn. There were three medical board interviewers. One of them was a foreign medical physician. He had a middle-eastern accent.

He asked me, "How are you?"

I replied, "I am fine and you?"

Our conversation continued for about five minutes.

He said, "Thank you for coming."

I was terrified. Perhaps, they failed me!

I asked the medical board interviewers with curiosity, "What do you mean, thank you for coming?"

The medical board interviewers smiled and said to me, "You're done! We just wanted to know if you could speak English and converse with patients!"

I was overwhelmed and thanked each interviewer.

And then one added, "We will send your medical licensure certificate in the mail within 30 days."

I picked up my notebook and strolled out of the room as fast as I could. I thanked God and my father for their blessings. Tears of joy poured from my eyes. I couldn't help it; my heart was thundering through my chest wall with joy and excitement. I couldn't believe that it was finally over, and that my wish had been granted! Choua was waiting anxiously in the waiting room.

She exclaimed, "What was going on?"

I told her the great news. She gave me a hug and said, "You did it, Honey!" We were grateful and ecstatic! We drove home, our hearts warm with joy and satisfaction. The wait for the next chapter in our lives began.

Residency Call Room—Afraid of the Living

One night, Choua came to have dinner with me and then stayed overnight in our resident call room. Our resident call room was small and very cozy. There was a couch with a pull-up bed and a study desk. While Choua fell asleep, I was paged to go downstairs to pronounce a patient's death in the intensive care unit. When I came back to the room, Choua was fearful. She told me that a man wearing white clothes had come into the room and put his hands over her mouth. She couldn't breathe or scream. Suddenly, she managed to open her eyes and no one was there. She was scared and wanted to leave! As for myself, I was not afraid of the dead or ghosts. I was more afraid of the living.

Interviewing as a Licensed Medical Doctor

I had an interview to practice as a Family Physician in Manitowoc, Wisconsin, in February of 2008. Choua and I made the trip and the clinic booked us a huge executive suite in a luxury hotel on the lakefront. We were so excited and jumped on the bed! There was an expensive bottle of wine on the table, and a large beautiful fruit basket with my name on a card—"Welcome, Dr. Xa Xiong, MD". We were overjoyed. Choua asked if the wine was free.

I said, "I don't care! Just drink it!"

During the contract negotiation process, they offered me an exceptional sign-on bonus, moving expenses, and an annual 6-figure salary.

Without hesitation, we said, "We'll take it!"

I signed the contract before I actually finished my residency. We went back to Manitowoc one month later to search for our new home. We found a beautiful four-bedroom house and dedicated this new home to my parents. Although my father was no longer here to live with us I knew deep down in my heart that he would be very happy. It was perfect—with a yard big enough for a soccer field.

Graduating from Medical Residency

Finally the time came for graduation. I was most thankful to God for giving me the opportunity of a lifetime and for making the seemingly impossible dream become a reality. I thanked my dad, my mom, my aunt, my wife, my kids, my teachers, my mentors, my attending physicians, all the wonderful nurses and staff at UW Health Fox Valley Family Medicine, Appleton Medical Center, St. Elizabeth Hospital, and those who believed in me and even those who doubted me. Without them, I would not have fulfilled my dream. The graduation was an evening I had longed for my entire life.

My mom said to me, "This is what your father wanted. Even though he is not here physically, he is with us spiritually and he is very happy."

My father was always with me in my heart.

I thanked God for bringing us safely to America from Laos, and for protecting my family and me during our separations. I was able to experience the traveling of a lifetime: California, St. Lucia Island, Mexico, Texas, Arizona, and Alaska. Now, at last, we could move forward. It was a long journey on a rocky road, but we made it. The fortune teller was right about Choua's future. She had married me and made a doctor out of me.

Moving to Manitowoc, Wisconsin

We moved to Manitowoc on June 30, 2008. Our new home was 4,500 square feet with 3.5 acres of land on which we made a soccer field. Our new home had four bedrooms, three full bathrooms, a half bath, and a master bedroom with a full bath, jacuzzi, shower, and two sinks. The house had an open concept kitchen, an island in the center with two sinks and a large pantry. There was a remote three-car garage and a fully furnished basement with a large living room, a bar, refrigerator, pool table, and a large recreation room. Choua had her own laundry room. I had an office to myself on the first floor and a rather large sunroom with surrounding windows exposing a beautiful view. We had everything we could ever wish for! We were happy and the kids were happy with their new rooms and bathrooms that they did not have to share with others. The kids had their own television with cable, games, bookshelves and everything they needed. They struggled while I pursued my dream. Now I wanted to give them the world.

I provided medical care to all ages, from newborns to 106-year-olds. Our lives were fulfilled and we could not ask for more. This did not last long, however. I started to realize that although we had everything we needed at the moment, but there was still more that needed to be accomplished.

Choua and I had a bucket list that we wanted to accomplish, and the first thing on that list was to have a celebration party to thank God and the people who had helped us. We hosted a grand celebration at the Holiday Inn in Manitowoc on August 8, 2008. More than two hundred and fifty people came to the party. The food was excellent and everyone dressed up formally! Everyone we anticipated was there, except for my father, who would have been the happiest man on earth. I gave a speech, thanking my parents for their perseverance and for supporting me all the way. I thanked them for believing in me. I had tears running down my face because my father could not be with me to celebrate this joyous moment. Instead we dedicated a chair for my father and thanked him for always believing in me and for all the sacrifices he made to give me a good life. I thanked my mom for being the best mother a son could ever have, for giving birth to me and for always loving me no matter what. I thanked my in-laws for giving birth to Choua, who fully supported me through all the hardships that we went through. Without her, I would not have succeeded. I thanked my aunt, Shoua Kue, for taking care of our children and for keeping our home warm while I was gone to medical school and during my residency program. I thanked everyone for their support, those who believed in me, and those who doubted me. Most of importantly, Choua and I thanked God for giving us the ability, perseverance, love, and blessing to make our seemingly impossible dream become the possible dream.

I continued the quest to help the Hmong people and dedicated my life to care for others. I was invited by many organizations across the United States to be a keynote speaker on various topics ranging from how to pursue higher education to leadership, finances, and family counseling. One of the most unforgettable moments took place on December 4, 2009. A few weeks prior, I had been invited by the president of the Hmong Laos Family Community Center in Milwaukee, as a guest speaker with General Vang Pao on the topic of mental health as it affected the Hmong community.

After the speech I was invited by General Vang Pao to sit at his table, and have dinner with him and his wife. I sat across from the general.

He said, "It would be a great honor for you to have dinner with us."

He began to place his food on my plate. The general's wife, Song Moua, took a piece of boiled chicken leg and placed it on my plate.

The general took his freshly made rice (mov nplej tshab) and put it on my plate, and said, "Eat, my son."

I replied in a nervous tone, "Thank you."

It was truly an honor to have a meal and a casual conversation with the general and his wife. If my father was still here, he would be sitting next to me and would be proud. On the inside I could feel my father's happiness.

Shortly after dinner, I brought my mother over to meet General Vang Pao and his wife. He complimented my father and my mother for being excellent parents. He told my mother, "Captain Yong Ge Xiong was a great man, a leader and a kind hearted person...his legacy will never be forgotten." I thanked him from the bottom of my heart. It was a dream comes true for me, my father, my mother, my wife, and my children.

My mother broke down in tears and told me, "That was your father's dream." I broke down in tears and thanked my father and my mother for everything they had done for me. The evening ended quickly but with much satisfaction and happiness. We stayed in a hotel in Milwaukee that night.

The next morning we attended the Milwaukee Hmong New Year Celebration. More than two thousand people attended that year. Upon the arrival of General Vang Pao, I was invited to walk next to him and the other leaders to cut the ceremonial ribbon for the opening of the New Year celebration. I was standing behind him and listened to him closely as he blessed the New Year and everyone with good health, wealth and prosperity. As I listened carefully, I had a vision—a vision that may be distant and impossible but if I work hard enough, one day, I will be invited to cut the ceremonial ribbon just like the general. This vision was immediately imprinted in my conscious mind.

Shortly after General Vang Pao gave his speech to thousands of Hmong people, I was introduced by the emcee to give a short speech. My speech was to commemorate General Vang Pao for his words of wisdom.

He had spoken these words to me twenty-three years ago and I proclaimed them to the crowd, "…pursue higher education and help other people. Then life will be good and prosperous."

I thanked him for his words of wisdom and promised to continue his legacy for future generations. He blessed me with his own words of wisdom for endless prosperity and fruitfulness in my future medical practice. It was truly an honor and a moment of a lifetime.

I have been invited as a keynote speaker and have given hundreds of speeches for various occasions, community events, conferences and school graduations. I was listed as one of the five accomplished Hmong Americans in the book, *The Hmong: Coming to America* by Kaarin Alisa, 2007. I co-authored a chapter book *Ethnicity and the Dementias—Working with Hmong-American Families*, which provided cultural information for healthcare providers working with Hmong clients experiencing dementia. I was invited as one of the keynote speakers for The Wisconsin 35th Hmong Refugee Anniversary: Mental Health Facing the Hmong Community in Sheboygan in 2010.

During that same year I was also invited to teach a Webinar at Stanford University on the topic of Ethnicity and Dementias among Hmong American Families.

On January 31, 2011, I was elected as one of the honorable keynote speakers by the Hmong senior leaders in Wisconsin to represent the Hmong youth at the candle light ceremony honoring General Van Pao in Appleton, Wisconsin. On June 18th, 2011 I received the "Journey of Hope Award" by Secretary Eloise Anderson from the Wisconsin Department of Children and Families, "for outstanding achievement by a refugee during resettlement and integration into American society."

I became an active member in the Manitowoc Hmong community; helping the community to prosper, providing medical care with cultural competence, mediating political issues, and resolving conflicts. I built a strong relationship with the mayor of Manitowoc, Mr. Justin Nickels. During my Honorary Achievement and Blessing Ceremony on August 20, 2011, Mayor Justin Nickels was one of the guest speakers and presented me with a "COMMENDATION" award. It was truly an honor!

The promise I made to my brother many years ago was finally fulfilled! The dream that my father and mother had longed for had become a reality. The impossible dream that Choua and I had suffered and fought for became the possible dream. The pinnacle of academic success had been reached and commemorated with a flag of victory. However, there was more to life than simply achieving an impossible dream. The lowest point of my life was when I was studying for the final Family Medicine Board Certification Examination through the American Board of Family Medicine. This exam was not an ordinary one where you'd study for a week and take it in one go. It took time to master the material in order to pass the exam. I had put in countless hours throughout the years to study while working as a full time physician. I was very nervous and had many fears of failing the exam.

My exam was schedule in Madison, Wisconsin. I took a week off of work prior to the board exam and literally lived in a hotel near Madison to finish my studies with the little time I had left. The day before the board exam, I was studying in a bookstore on the west side. I was completely exhausted from studying so I decided to stand up and take a stroll through the bookstore. I was searching for any book that would motivate and inspire me to study for my board. As I came to the inspirational section I saw Jack Canfield— *The Success Principles.* His picture was on the front cover and he was charismatically smiling at me. I took his book off the shelf and started reading it. From then on I couldn't take my eyes off the pages. I spent four hours straight reading his book while standing by the book shelf.

When I read Principle 5, "*BELIEVE IN YOUR-SELF*—You must choose to believe that you can do anything you set your mind to—anything at all—because, in fact, you can."[2] My attitude was completely changed for the better. An abundance of energy and confidence surged through my body and mind. I didn't study the rest of the afternoon. I bought Jack Canfield's *The Success Principles,* and continued to read throughout the rest of the day.

The next day, I took my board exam and the rest is history. I scored well and passed the most stressful exam I have ever taken in my life. *The Success Principles* by Jack Canfield became one of the two most important books in my life, second only to the Bible. I shared the book with my wife and my children and they all loved it. I was then determined to meet Jack Canfield in person so I could express my gratitude and thank him for giving me positive affirmation.

God has blessed me with the ability to restore lives and the privilege of serving my community. There is no such thing as spare time, because every second is another opportunity for a difference to be made. As a leader and provider, I am actively involved in different organizations and have served as a board member, director, advisor, chair, president, vice-president, and consultant. When I reflect on my life, I could not be more content as I continue to climb to the pinnacle of my service and success.

One of the most cherished moments in my life was honoring over 80 Wisconsin Lao-Hmong Veterans with the Benevolent Medal of Honor for their sacrifice and bravery during the Vietnam/Secret War in Laos. My family and I acknowledged the men and women for being the key to opening the door to new opportunities as we continue our life journey in America. Their smiles in return filled my heart with warmth, giving my life a new purpose.

Recently, my five children, Choua and I visited the Hmong Language and Culture Enrichment Program (HLCEP) in Madison with students ranging from ages 5 to 14. As a family, we created a workshop incorporating medical games and activities to educate the students about the importance of the cardiovascular system, living a healthy lifestyle and achieving higher education. Our goal was to motivate the children to dream bigger, live healthier and pursue education as a lifetime investment. I remember the voice of a ten-year-old boy who exclaimed, "Dr. Xiong, you must be very rich and have a lot of money!" I was startled and surprised from his comment.

Before I could respond to the little boy, the program director replied, "Dr. Xiong has a very rich heart."

I was very touched and told the young boy, "Education will make you a rich person."

To commemorate the New Year, I was invited to cut

the 2014-2015 New Year's ribbon in Wausau, Wisconsin. This was truly an unexpected honor that I will treasure for the rest of my life. The ribbon ceremony welcomes the New Year for all families and friends with new beginnings and blessings. It was a dream comes true as I had envisioned when I was with General Vang Pao several years before.

As citizens of the United States of America, we should be proud to make this country ours. We should acknowledge the beautiful diverse cultures, abide by the laws, and achieve the American dream. The American dream is to reach prosperity and success, accomplished through hard work, and achieve the highest levels *of individual health, leadership, income, family, and education*—known as *i*LIFE.

CHAPTER TEN

*i*LIFE Pearls

iLIFE Pearls

After many years of pursuing higher education, practicing as a family physician, being in the position of leadership, reaching the pinnacle of success, and motivating others to reach their own dreams, the acronym *i*LIFE is practiced in my own life every day. As I continue onto the next milestone in life I would very much like to help individuals who are prepared to work hard to achieve their impossible dreams. Those who have a resilient vision and robust determination can make the seemingly impossible dream become a reality through the practice of *i*LIFE. With a little encouragement and guidance, anyone can succeed beyond their imaginations.

The world is always changing rapidly. We have to adapt to the changes, both socially and economically, or else we will fall behind. In the 1980's, we had spinning dial phones with long extension cords that connected to the wall; huge stationary IBM computers that you could hardly lift off the table; talking Apple Macintosh computers; Michael Jackson, the King of Pop; *"Pretty in Pink,"* the best teenager love movie ever made; and Michael J. Fox in *"Back to the Future."*

Today, we have the iPad, iPod, iPhone, iComputer, YouTube, Twitter, Instagram, Pinterest, Face-book, Snapchat, Tumblr, etc. You get the idea. Since the world is changing rapidly, we must adapt and prepare ourselves for ultimate life challenges. Today, we live in a competitive world that requires goal directives, perseverance, endurance, and a commitment to self-discipline in order to succeed in life.

After many years of pursuing higher education and overcoming life crises, I have come up with a new word called **iLIFE**, which consists of five elements. The *i* simply stands for *individual health* by staying in a harmonious physical, mental, and spiritual well-being. The **L** stands for leadership. The **I** stands for income. The **F** stands for family. The **E** stands for education. Each of the elements represents 20 percent of an individual's life force and when adding all of them together, it becomes 100 percent. *i*LIFE begins with the chronological order of family, *individual health,* education, income and leadership. In order to succeed in each of the elements, an individual must have a clear vision and pursue self-actualization to the fullest magnitude.

FAMILY

Family is defined as a specific group of people made up of a husband, wife, and children. A healthy family begins with you. It is essential to love your spouse and your children as you love your own body. Each individual has his/her own love cell that needs constant filling in order for the cell to remain healthy. Based on research, when we are dating, we are in a euphoric love period, and this time compels a person to be blinded by love. It reminds me one of the lyrics in a song, "I will catch the grenade for you." Research has shown that after two years of marriage, the euphoric love period starts to slowly disappear, and some-times we don't even want to catch our own grenade. We need to continue to feed our love cell so our euphoric love for each other can be long-lasting until death do us part. We must love our spouse the way we want to be loved. We can fill our spouse's love cell every day by following what I call, "The Five Principles of Marriage":

1. **_Understanding Love._** What is love? From a medical standpoint, love is the most powerful neural system in the body. Love involves numerous neurotransmitters in the central nervous system such as: Adrenaline—a neurotrans-mitter that activates the body's stress response that leads to increased heart rates, sweating, and dry mouth; Dopamine—causes a desire and reward effect by triggering an intense rush of pleasure having the same effect on the brain as taking cocaine; and Serotonin—causes loved ones to keep popping into your thoughts. These neurotransmitters activate the neuron cells to excite a state of mind in a euphoric love mode. Love is the essence of our body cells' life. Love is good for health. Research shown that happily married people, in the long term, suffer less

depression and live significantly longer than those who are single, divorced, or widowed. Love reduces the risk of mental illness and physical problems. Love reduces the risk of family conflicts and builds a stronger family bond. Love reduces the risk of divorce. Love overcomes life's obstacles. Love increases prosperity and wealth.

Things we do to maintain and improve our love life:

- Love your spouse as though you only have three days to live.
- Don't be afraid to say "I love you."
- Be 100 percent faithful in marriage.
- Be respectful and provide 100 percent support to your spouse. Men, help your wives with doing the dishes, cleaning the toilet, taking out the trash, etc. Women, help your husbands with washing the car, mowing the lawn, ironing clothes, fixing the car, etc.
- Don't be afraid to admit your mistakes, and say "I'm sorry."
- Take time out when issues get heated.
- Before reacting angrily, count one to ten and take a deep breath.
- Surprise your spouse with thoughtfulness by giving a special gift.
- Spend good quality time together and make every minute count. Life is short.
- Don't forget to send flowers to your spouse and say "I love you."

2. **Keep Commitment.** There are seven billion people in the world. Marriage is the ultimate life decision to be committed exclusively to one person, by making a vow of matrimony with each other over all others. This signifies that you are not married by chance but by the grace of God and Mother Nature. The wedding ring is an unbroken circle that has a smooth inner surface that never ends and is normally worn over the left fourth finger. Prior to medical science, people believed that a vein ran directly from the left fourth finger to the heart. In medicine, the left fourth finger is called *"digitus medicinalis"*. In Latin, the vein that connects from the left fourth finger to the heart is called the *"vena amoris"*, the vein of love. In many cultures, the ring worn over the left fourth finger represents eternal commitment and love. Happy marriage requires 100 percent commitment from each person and there are NO exceptions. The gravel has been struck with no further discussion. The envelope has been sealed.

3. **Give Praise.** Words of encouragement are very powerful. They activate the conscious and subconscious mind that influence one's self-worth and emotions. The repetition of telling your spouse, "I love you, honey, my sweetheart; you look good, you are beautiful, you are the love of my life; I can't live without you, I can't wait to see you, I can't wait to come home; and thank you," makes the partner feel valued, appreciated and loved.

4. ***Stay Young.*** One must continue to stay young. Remember we must continue to live with euphoric love and never let it disappear. To stay young is like food that needs added spice to make it taste good. It is the duty of a married couple to continue to add spice to their marriage. Marriage spice ingredients are bountiful hugs, affectionate kisses, gentle passion, and intimacy, holding hands, massaging each other's shoulders and feet, and spending quality time together. Quality time means keeping 100 percent full attention on your spouse. One piece of advice I have been giving to many people is to keep cuddling each other or otherwise someone else will be cuddling you or your spouse. The bottom line is to continue filling up your spouse's love cell and never let it empty. So give it a try tonight. Buy your spouse a dozen roses and say, "Honey, I love you and you mean the world to me." It may transform your relationship for the better forever.

5. ***Protect the Marriage.*** A married couple should build their own *family circle of trust* with a circular steel wall and steel roof to protect the marriage. The family circle of trust should only have a small door to fit an individual in and out. The door should be guarded at all times and other people should not be allowed to get through the door or break the steel wall. The family circle of trust can be secured by what I call, "The Five Avoiding Principles."

> ***Avoiding Principle One*** – Avoid accepting personal gifts from anyone of the opposite sex who is

not in your family circle of trust. Giving a personal gift may send a wrong message.

Avoiding Principle Two – Avoid private conversations with anyone of the opposite sex who is not in your family circle of trust. Having a private lunch or dinner may signify the initiating a relationship.

Avoiding Principle Three – Avoid physical touch with anyone of the opposite sex who is not in your family circle of trust. Physical touch may send a wrong message to the brain which interprets it as a sign of love and affection.

Avoiding Principle Four – Avoid cyberspace contact, such as chatting on Facebook or private emailing with anyone of the opposite sex who is not in your family circle of trust. This may develop a cyberspace relationship and may lead to a destructtive relationship.

Avoiding Principle Five – Avoid disclosing your personal marital problems with anyone of the opposite sex who is not in your family circle of trust. Disclosing your marital problems with others may open the door of the family circle of trust for intruders to step in. The marriage could end in catastrophe.

Precious Gifts

The role of a parent is to promote and support the physical, emotional, social, and intellectual development of a child from infancy to adulthood. Children are precious gifts. Parents are indebted to give love, provide protection and assist with building the child's future. Parents, don't forget to give love to your children. Not only giving love but giving respect as well. Parents are teachers and should be teaching the children the right scheme of life by being a good role model, being a good and true friend to your children, and building a close relationship with the children. In this way, the children will feel more connected to you, will trust you, and will come back to you if they should have a need or a problem.

Parents give life to children. In return, children must give love and respect to parents. Parents are doctors, nurses, teachers, counselors, encouragers, protectors, and bankers. Parents give shelter, strength, direction, and sweet security when children are lost. Parents help children to fly when their wings are broken. Parents are worth more than twelve million dollars (each parent is six million dollars) and there is no replacement. All parents ask from the children is to give back love and respect by being a noble person, being a moral student, pursuing higher education and becoming a doctor, lawyer, or engineer. Children should wake up early in the morning, help out with the house chores, and not spend too much time on the cell phone, playing video games or being on Facebook. Life is short and time cannot be wasted.

INDIVIDUAL HEALTH

Each human is born with 23 pairs of chromosomes or a total of 46 chromosomes. One copy of the each chromosome is inherited from the mother and the other from the father. There are sex chromosomes that differentiate females from males; females have two X chromosomes and males have one X and one Y chromosome. There are fifty trillion tiny cells in the body and each cell contains a nucleus that consists of DNA (deoxyribonucleic acid) with a complete set of encoded instructions. The DNA is organized into chromosomes. Chromosomes organize into genes. Genes make proteins that determine who we are. Scientists have found that humans have 99.5 percent genetic similarity and only 0.5 percent difference. Scientists have also found that our chromosomes or DNA can be altered by gene mutation that has varied effects on health and alters the role of essential cell functions. Mutated genes affect health, causing illness to develop.

You must take full responsibility of your own life and remain in harmony and in good health—physically, mentally, and spiritually. Without that, you will not be able to care for yourself, your spouse, your children, your parents, your siblings, nor the community. You must love and respect your own body 100 percent. You must take full responsibility for your own actions to keep yourself physically, psychologically, and spiritually healthy at all times.

You are an important person to yourself, your spouse, and your children.

Medical conditions that are rising in the world today are cardiovascular disease, diabetes, hypertension, hyperlipidemia, lung cancer, stomach and colon cancer, and mental health illnesses such as depression, anxiety, post-traumatic stress disorder, bipolar disorder, and schizophrenia. Research has shown that 65 percent of all deaths in adults are caused by heart disease, cancer, and/or stroke. In most of the cases, these diseases can be prevented.

If you have a medical condition, it is strongly advised that you seek medical expertise immediately. You should not be afraid to see a healthcare provider, get an annual physical exam, obtain blood or imaging testing, take your medications as prescribed daily, and/or have surgery to remove the causes of your medical condition(s) if necessary. The healthcare provider is there to support you, to help you with your medical decisions, to extend your life, and not to perform experiments on you. Actually doctors are more afraid of you than you are of them.

You must take full action now to prevent diseases from developing in the future. I have written 10 self-discipline principles that may help you to stay physically, mentally, and spiritually healthy;

1. Maintain a healthy weight. Keep track of your weight on a routine basis. If you are overweight, you should take the initiative not to gain any more weight.

2. Eat a healthy diet. Eat a diet that is rich in fruits, vegetables, whole grains, and keep red meat to a minimum. Eat small-portioned meals several times a day instead of one or two big meals. Taking a multi-vitamin that contains folate daily is a great supplement for the body.

3. Exercise regularly. Exercise daily for 30-60 minutes and make exercise a daily routine. Choose an exercise that you enjoy performing or stay motivated by exercising with someone.

4. If you smoke, STOP! There are many programs and treatments available. Your family doctor can help you to quit smoking.

5. If you drink alcohol, keep it to a minimum. It is recommended to limit consumption to 2 drinks (one drink is equal to 1 can of 12 oz. beer, one 4 oz. glass of wine, or 1.5 oz. of liquor). I strongly recommend drinking NO alcohol if you are pregnant or trying to get pregnant. Do not drink while you are operating a vehicle or other equipment. Alcohol is known to cause interruption in the brain cells, which leads to both acute and chronic cognitive and memory impairments. You should avoid alcohol intake if you are taking other medications without your physician's knowledge.

6. Connect with others. Get involved with churches or your community. This will give you a sense of connection with reality, self-esteem and a decrease in mental health issues.

7. Serve others. Volunteer time to do something for someone. Look for opportunities to serve others, paying someone a compliment or donating money to charity. This will make you feel good with the added bonus of making someone else feel good too.

8. Enhance positive thinking ability. Develop a habit of positive thinking instead of negative thinking. This will result in lower blood pressure, lower heart rate, and increased blood flow to the brain and other organs.

9. Prevent yourself from contracting communicable diseases. You can protect yourself by being abstinent from sexual activity or remain in a committed monogamous relationship.

10. Get an annual physical examination and routine screening tests. Annual routine blood tests may include complete blood count, basic metabolic panel, liver function test, lipid panel, and hemocult (stool test for blood). There are a number of important screenings and tests that can help to detect cancer early in females such as a mammogram (breast cancer), colonoscopy (colorectal cancer), pap smear (cervical cancer), ovarian cancer screening, and skin cancer screening. For males there are colonoscopy (colorectal cancer), prostate specific antigen (prostate cancer) and skin cancer screening. Lung cancer in both males and females can be detected through low-dose computed

tomography (low dose-CT scan or LDCT) and is recommended for people who have a history of heavy smoking, smoke now, or have quit within the past 15 years and are between 55 and 80 years old.

EDUCATION

Genetically speaking, everyone is born with the genes of education (desire to learn), knowledge, and wisdom. These genes are encoded in our DNA and are passed to us by our parents. As stated before, each individual is made up of forty-six chromosomes, and the only difference between man and woman are the X and Y chromosomes. This means that we have 99.5 percent genetic similarity and only 0.5 percent difference. If other people can achieve *LIFE*, so can you. You are capable of achieving any high level of education, earning multiple doctorate degrees, choosing the lifestyle you want to live, and being the person you want to be. There will be times that your energy will be low; there will be times when other people try to discourage you from reaching your destiny. There will be times of troubles, times of sickness, major obstacles to overcome, financial difficulty and family sacrifices to be made. No matter how many times you fail in life, never, never, never give up. Keep pressing forward. If you do, one day you will succeed. The bottom line is you are capable of unlocking the treasures of life in the universe.

One of the comments that was made after one of my

speeches was, "I was born to a non-educated family and it is in my bloodline. It would be impossible for me to learn and get a high education." My answer to this comment is that you are encoded with the desire to learn and it is in your bloodline. You can be the first in your bloodline to get an education and be the first one to become a doctor, lawyer or engineer.

Five reasons why most people don't succeed in achieving higher education:

1. It never occurs to them that education is an important part of life.
2. Failure to recognize that higher education is achievable.
3. Failure to initiate the decision to pursue higher education.
4. Procrastination excuses such as blaming age, family issues, or financial problems.
5. Fear of being a failure.

It is important to understand that *"education is a collection of knowledge that makes up a master key to open many doors in life."* It can open the doors of knowledge, health, wealth, and prosperity. As we know, the majority of parents want their children to become doctors, lawyers, engineers, or have high-paying jobs.

Some of the famous quotes that have inspired me to succeed in higher education are:

"Education is the key to becoming a successful person."
—Captain Yong Ge Xiong (my father)

"...pursue higher education and help other people. Then life will be good and prosperous,"
—General Vang Pao

"No matter what you want to do with your life, I guarantee that you will need an education to do it."
—President Barack Obama

As our forefathers have so perfectly spoken, we should pursue education to the fullest extent by achieving the highest level of education.

There are five levels of education that I have developed to serve as a guide known as the Educational Cascade Model. (Figure 1.)

- Level I Completed high school diploma
- Level II Completed bachelor's degree
- Level III Completed master's degree
- Level IV Completed doctoral degree
- Level V Completed postdoctoral degree in area of specialty

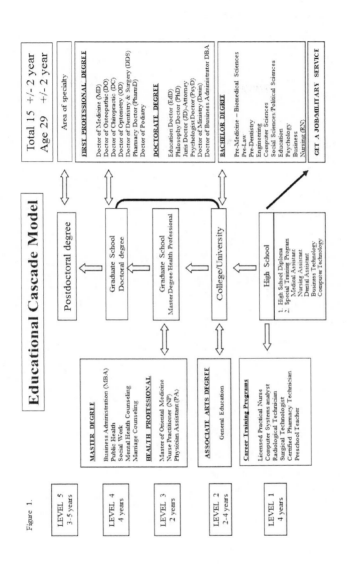

Figure 1.

Educational Cascade Model

Total 15 +/- 2 year
Age 29 +/- 2 year

Area of specialty

FIRST PROFESSIONAL DEGREE

Doctor of Medicine (MD)
Doctor of Osteopathic (DO)
Doctor of Chiropractic (DC)
Doctor of Optometry (OD)
Doctor of Dentistry & Surgery (DDS)
Pharmacy Doctor (PharmD)
Doctor of Podiatry

DOCTORATE DEGREE

Education Doctor (EdD)
Philosophy Doctor (PhD)
Juris Doctor (JD)-Attorney
Psychologist Doctor (PsyD)
Doctor of Ministry (Dmin)
Doctor of Business Administrator DBA

BACHELOR DEGREE

Pre-Medicine – Biomedical Sciences
Pre-Law
Pre-Dentistry
Engineering
Computer Sciences
Social Sciences Political Sciences
Education
Psychology
Business
Nursing (RN)

GET A JOB/MILITARY SERVICE

Postdoctoral degree

Graduate School
Doctoral degree

Graduate School
Master Degree Health Professional

College/University

High School

1. High School Diploma
2. Special Training Program
   Medical Assistant
   Nursing Assistant
   Dental Assistant
   Business Technology
   Computer Technology

MASTER DEGREE

Business Administration (MBA)
Public Health
Social Work
Mental Health Counseling
Marriage Counseling

HEALTH PROFESSIONAL

Master of Oriental Medicine
Nurse Practitioner (NP)
Physician Assistant (PA)

ASSOCIATE ARTS DEGREE

General Education

Career Training Programs

Licensed Practical Nurse
Computer Systems analyst
Radiological Technician
Surgical Technologist
Certified Pharmacy Technician
Preschool Teacher

LEVEL 5
3-5 years

LEVEL 4
4 years

LEVEL 3
2 years

LEVEL 2
2-4 years

LEVEL 1
4 years

It is vital to understand each level of education and have a clear vision with an abundance of dedication and perseverance to pursue life to the fullest potential.

It is extremely important to be educated and have an advance visionary goal at an early age. My Educational Cascade Model is designed to serve as a Future Global Navigating System (FGNS) to guide an individual to reach his or her visionary destination in a reasonable amount of time. My Educational Cascade Model worked for me to achieve my visionary goals and be who I am today. Each of our children has their own Educational Cascade Model that we have designed specifically for each individual. Our first daughter graduated from college at age 21 and is currently a fourth year medical student. Our second and third children are pursuing their biomedical sciences degrees and are in the process of studying for their Medical College Admission Test (MCAT). Our youngest daughter is a junior in high school and planning to attend medical school right after high school. Our youngest son is also planning to attend medical school in the near future as well. It is never too early to be educated and have an advance clear visionary goal. Remember this: you are already encoded with the genes of education and you will succeed to the highest level if you don't give up. Keep pressing forward and one day you shall succeed.

Things that can cause a physiological and psychological response in activating the genes of education are:

1. Attending school
2. Exposure to educational seminar and conference
3. Seeking advice from mentors, parents, educators, Pastors, leaders, and teachers
4. Living in a good environment and eating nutritious meals
5. Having an advance visionary goal—Future Global Navigating System (FGNS)

Things that can cause a physiological or psychological response in deactivating the genes of education are:

1. Smoking, alcohol, and drugs. These substances are found to disrupt brain function.
2. Mental health disorders: depression, PTSD, and genetic disorders.
3. Physical health disorders: severe head trauma, infection, stroke and dementia.
4. Spiritual disorders: spiritual warfare, soul loss, and demonic possession

Educators are lifelong readers. My Spanish teacher in High School, Mr. Espinosa, always reminded me to read, "Read anything you want." Reading is an exercise to the mind as physical exercise is to the body. The more you read, the more knowledge you will attain. Everyone is busy with life, but "I don't have enough time to read," is not a valid excuse. Do you use the toilet daily? The answer is yes! We spend at least 10 minutes three times daily to use the toilet to empty our body waste. This amounts to 30 minutes a day. Use these 30 minutes to read, call it "Toilet Reading." Imagine this: If you read 30 minutes each day and multiply it by seven days, you will read over 210 minutes, which is equivalent to 3.5 hours per week. Multiply that by 52 weeks and you will spend 182 hours reading and learning new information annually. In 10 years, you will accumulate 1820 hours. My advice is to read at least one book a month and in one year, you will have read 12 books, and in 10 years 120 books. This will give you an advantage over people who are less informed about the world and will have a major impact on your career.

One of the most important keys to success is the continuation of active learning. Active learning is a process of engaging in activities that involve reading, writing, discussion, teaching, or problem solving. Active learning can strengthening your short term and long term memory process so you can retain things more effectively and can improve your performance on tests and excel in school. After being a student for more than 40 years, and taking hundreds of tests, I have found active learning to be very effective.

There are several active learning tips that I have developed and used throughout my learning.

1. Go to class daily, take good notes, engage in class participation and ask questions.
2. Choose a study place that is free from noises and distractions. An example would be your nearby library.
3. Make reading a daily habit, review class notes regularly, and review old test questions if available.
4. Make note cards, create mnemonics, and highlight important parts with color highlighters.
5. Take breaks. Read or study for 50 minutes then take a 10 minute break. This will help refresh your memory bank so you can learn more.

My top 10 bullet points for succeeding in school:

1. Learn to activate the genes of education.
2. Be goal directed. Choose a lifelong habit of learning and enlarging your vision as you pursue your goal.
3. Stay with the people who lift you up, not drag you down.
4. Wake up early and plan your daily schedule. Go to class early, and do extra study and reading. Be well prepared for exams. Do not cram.
5. Seek advice from mentors, teachers, classmates, friends and parents. Don't act like you know everything, because there are a lot of things that we still don't know.
6. Use physical and educational activities to relieve stress: participate in competitive sport activities,

attend educational seminars and conferences, eat a healthy diet that is rich in fruits, vegetables and whole grains, keeping red meat to a minimum and make 30 to 60 minutes of exercise a daily habit.

7. Avoid drugs and alcohol. Research has shown that drug and alcohol can interfere with brain cells and cause interference of neurotransmitters, which leads to memory loss and cognitive impairment. It can also cause liver failure and liver cancer. Avoid cigarette smoking, which is the number one cause for major medical conditions such as cardiovascular disease, lung cancer, stroke, etc.

8. Avoid gambling and high-risk activities such as diving, snowboarding, rock climbing, and car racing.

9. If you should fail, try again (and again, if necessary) and you shall succeed.

10. Never, never, never quit.

To sum up, education is the master key that opens many doors in life. It's a lifetime investment, and it is power. No dream is too big. If you can dream it, you can achieve it through education. As long as you stay hungry for knowledge, there is nothing that you cannot achieve. Keep pressing forward, keep seeking, keep asking, keep using your abilities to bring out the best in yourself and you shall receive.

INCOME

Income represents 20 percent of the *i*LIFE force. Choua and I always pictured ourselves among the top 1 percent income earners, but it was never easy. Every day we faced numerous financial difficulties just like everyone else did, but we believed that we could earn a high income and become wealthy. In the past, we barely had enough money to cover our expenses. We lived paycheck to paycheck and were not even able to cover our monthly expenses. We worked hard to understand the financial world and asked ourselves, "Why do people get rich and how did they do it?" We read numerous money maker magazines, fortune magazines, and other types of financial books. Many hours of reading gave us insight to develop an equation that helped us understand the logic of earning a high income.

High Education Level + High Wage Job - Taxes = High Income.

In today's world, everyone is competing for high paying jobs that require minimal physical labor. In order to receive a high paying salary an individual must have a high level of education that includes many hours of work, training and experience. It is imperative to obtain a high level of education, so achieving level 5 (postdoctoral degree) is highly recommended as discussed earlier in the Educational Cascade Model. If an individual's level of education is low, he or she may not be offered the job or will end up taking one paying only minimum wage and requiring laborious duties. For example, seeking a job as a dishwasher requires a low education level;

Low Education Level + Low Wage Job - Taxes = Low Income

The higher an individual's level of education, the greater the chance of being offered a high paying job. For example, seeking a job as a medical doctor requires a high level of education with many years of training and experience. With this in mind, Choua and I strove for a higher education level to begin with. It took me nineteen years to earn a bachelor's degree, a doctoral degree in chiropractic (DC), and a doctoral degree in medicine (MD).

Just achieving a high level of education along with a good socioeconomic status and a substantial income, is does not fulfill the income 20 percent of the *i*LIFE force. An individual or a couple must maintain their financial sustainability and know how to invest money wisely to fulfill the income 20 percent of the *i*LIFE force. Choua and I were financially secure but we were still living paycheck to paycheck even after earning a six-digit income. Our monthly expenses were more than what we earned each month. Choua and I began searching for solutions to our financial problems. Choua had a degree in accounting and understood financial investment better than I did. We spent many hours reading and researching to have a better understanding of the financial world. There are several financial terms that helped us solve our financial problems. (See Figure 2.)

- ***Income***—money flow into the bank account. This includes income and assets.
- ***Expenses***—money flow out of the bank account. This includes all expenses and liabilities.
- ***Liabilities***—debts owed, with or without interest.
- ***Assets***—wealth and possessions.

Once we understood those financial terms, we began to

Figure 2.

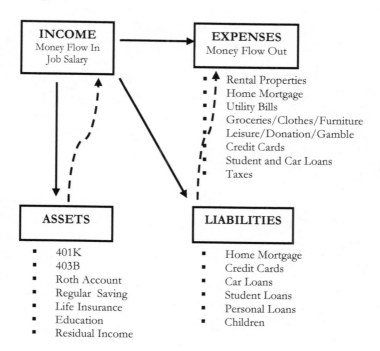

apply them to our financial troubles. The very first thing we did with each paycheck we received from work was take out 10 percent to pay ourselves. The other 90 percent was distributed among our expenses, liabilities, and assets. The 10 percent was deducted directly from our pay, tax-free, into our 403B account. Our employer matched up to a certain percentage on an annual basis, which compounded a lump sum of cash into the account. Over time, the result of our decision to change our financial difficulties was a positive financial accumulation.

We invested the other 90 percent in education (e.g., school tuition, room and board, attending educational conferences, and educating others), regular expenses, liability expenses, a life insurance policy, and a regular savings account. We minimized our expenses and liabilities by cutting down on leisure spending and vacationing, limiting the number of credit cards, and by buying a used car instead of a brand new one. We have applied the financial equation and the financial terms to our advantage and have been financially successful.

Another way of investing money is donating money to charities. Donating to worthy causes is a must. There are countless foundations and organizations in need of financial support to aid others. You must give in order to receive. If you give even a small sum of money to charities, God will reward you ten times what you put in if your heart is in the right place and you have compassion for others. Giving is a building block to your financial success.

Do not gamble. The chances of winning will diminish

the longer you play. The probability of winning is less than getting into a car accident or struck by lightning. Simply don't waste your time, money, or effort. You could be using your time, money, and effort to have a better chance at becoming a medical physician.

It is mandatory that you find the right way to save and invest money for your own advantage either by doing your own research, or by following our recommended path. The main objective for financial success is to minimize liabilities, cut expenses, maintain job income and accumulate assets.

LEADERSHIP

Leadership represents the last 20 percent of *i*LIFE force. Over the course of many years of being involved with a number of leadership positions, I have developed my leadership skills in a variety of ways. One way is through the opportunities I have had to shake hands with many different types of leaders. Each one has inspired me to become a more benevolent leader. A benevolent leader is someone who provides service with generosity and kindness rather than self-profit-making purposes. "Researchers found that 25 percent of the people you meet will not like you. The next 25 percent won't like you but could be persuaded to. Another 25 percent will like you but could be persuaded not to, and the final 25 percent will like you and stand by you no matter what."[5] This shows that, as leaders, we cannot expect to be 100 percent liked even if we desperately want to be.

As a leader, we should ask ourselves these three questions:

1. How can I help others in need of socioeconomic status improvement?

2. What can I do to inspire them to become better?

3. How can I make them feel more loved, more accepted, more valuable, more secure, and more productive?

Leaders of communities can rephrase John F. Kennedy's famous quote *"Ask not what your country can do for you, ask what you can do for your country,"* by stating, *"Ask not what your community can do for you, ask what you can do for your community."* This quote was incorporated into many of my speeches and was well received.

Leadership does not occur overnight, of course. It involves a long and treacherous process of hard work, dedication, and a positive attitude. Leaders must GROW over time. Leaders are learners, educators and listeners. I use the acronym GROW to exemplify the qualities of being an excellent leader.

The letter **G** stands for *Giving*. Let me give you an anecdote from my own experience that transformed me into a better leader. Several years ago, I was invited by a local organization to attend a summer festival. The organization was kind enough to send me several admission tickets, each worth three dollars. I was supposed to take the tickets and bring my family to attend the festival for free. We went to the festival and approached the admission gate. In front of us was an elderly man in his seventies.

The elderly man asked the young clerk, "How much does it cost to get into the festival?"

The young clerk replied, "Only three dollars!" And he added, "How old are you?"

The elder man replied, "Seventy years old."

The young clerk said, "If you are over sixty-five years old, you can go in for free."

But the man replied, "No, I have been saving money over the past year to come to this event. This event is only held once a year and I must pay to get in."

The young clerk demanded, "You can go for free!"

They conversed back and forth. The elderly man insisted that he should pay.

And then he said, "Consider this as a donation."

He handed three dollars to the surprised young clerk and he went into the festival park. At that moment I was holding my ticket and a sudden burst of realization came to mind, "I am a doctor who is financially secure. I can easily pay the three dollars. This is not right." I began to have heart palpitations, my palms started to sweat, and my face became florid.

I turned around and whispered to Choua, "We cannot do this."

We turned around and gave our tickets to others behind us so that they could go in for free. Then we got back in line and paid the full admission just like everyone else. What I learned from this elderly man was that leaders must learn how to give and to not take advantage of what is given to them. Sometimes we are blinded into not giving even though we have more than we need. We must give in order to receive. It doesn't matter how much we give. I know for sure that God, Mother Nature, and Ancestors will reward us ten times what we give to charities.

The **R** stands for *respect* and *reach out*. Leaders must give respect in order to be respected. Leaders must respect themselves, their spouses and their children. Leaders must respect others, including their supervisors, colleagues, staff and most importantly, the public. Leaders should reach out and build strong relationship with children, youths, adults, and elders. Excellent leaders have knowledge of the various personality types so that they can reach out with understanding to the people they encounter.

The **O** stands for *Openness*. Openness creates credibility and T.R.U.S.T;

- The T stands for *transparency* and *truthfulness*.
- The R stands for *reward* others.
- The U stands for the *unconditional* tender loving care for others.
- The S stands for *support* and *stimulation* of others to mold them into leaders.
- The T stands for *taking the lead* to inspire others to follow. My father always said, "Be a doer and not a talker."

The **W** stands for *working hard*. Leaders must go beyond their required duties. Leaders must be the first to arrive and the last to leave. Leaders must keep their commitment and not fail to achieve objectives and goals.

GROW empowers leaders to stay on track on the journey of life. Excellent, benevolent leaders will serve others with generosity and kindness rather choosing to be self-serving. Leaders should continue to grow, to serve others whole heartedly with humility and to inspire their many followers to achieve their own dreams.

As Dolly Parton, a famous country singer, actress, and inspiring philanthropist said, *"If your actions create a legacy that inspires others to dream more, learn more, do more, become more, then you are an excellent leader."*[1]

The Spouse of the Leader

The spouse of the leader is an important individual and has a major influence on the leader's success. A leader will fail his or her role as a leader if the spouse does not acquire the fundamental qualities of leadership to support his or her spouse. The following fundamental qualities can be implemented to enrich confidence between a leader and his or her spouse, and will have a significant impact on the general public's perception:

1. Have faith, respect and belief in your spouse as a leader.
2. Be supportive and elevate your spouse through

thick and thin circumstances.

3. Create a positive tone in the home and in public.
4. Be humble to serve and inspire others to follow.
5. Be a generous giver and kindhearted spouse.

These fundamental qualities will foster an atmosphere where leadership, encouragement, motivation, prosperity, love, and grace all flow together in harmony and result in fruitful leadership.

*i*LIFE is a continuous process that never ends. Choua and I continue to seek for knowledge to improve ourselves and to create a positive legacy for others to follow. We have an abundance of faith and believe in impossible dreams. We dream big and will continue to chase those dreams to the end. We dream of:

- becoming great philanthropists
- becoming amazing inspirational speakers
- creating an iMedical Career Program to plant seeds in young minds and give them insight into choosing to become health care providers
- meeting our inspirational role models such as Jack Canfield, Pastor Joel Osteen, President Barack Obama, and Oprah Winfrey within the next three years
- seeing our children become successful health care providers
- seeing this book made into a movie

Ten years from now, we expect to have succeeded in making our new impossible dreams become reality. In the end it will continue to be the American dream that we have always hoped for!

APPENDIX

ACRONYMS

i   *individual health*

L   LEADERSHIP

I   INCOME

F   FAMILY

E   EDUCATION

G   GIVING

R   RESPECT and REACH OUT

O   OPENNESS

W   WORKING HARD

T   TRANSPARENCY and TRUTHFULNESS

R   REWARD

U   UNCONDITIONAL TENDER LOVING CARE

S   SUPPORT and STIMULATION

T   TAKING THE LEAD

BIBLIOGRAPHY

1. Bethel, Sheila Murray, Ph.D. *A New Breed of Leader: 8 Leadership Qualities That Most In The Real World.* The Berkley Publishing Group and Penguin Group (USA) Inc. New York, 2009, page 94.
2. Canfield, Jack and Janet Switzer. *The Success Principles—How to Get from Where You Are to Where You Want to Be.* HarperCollins Publishers, Inc. New York, 2005, page 40.
3. Carson, Ben, MD. and Cecil Murphey. *Gifted Hands: The Ben Carson Story.* Review and Herald Publishing Association. Zondervan, Grand Rapids, Michigan, 1990.
4. Fadiman, Anne. *The Spirit Catches You and You Fall Down.* Farrar, Straus and Giroux. New York, 1997.
5. Osteen, Joel. *Every Day A Friday.* FaithWords-Hachette Book Group, Inc. New York, NY. 2011, page 78.

Made in the USA
Charleston, SC
14 May 2016